GOOGLE GEMINI

FOR

PYTHON

GOOGLE GEMINI

FOR

PYTHON

Coding with Bard

Oswald Campesato

MERCURY LEARNING AND INFORMATION
Boston, Massachusetts

Publisher: David Pallai
MERCURY LEARNING AND INFORMATION
121 High Street, 3rd Floor
Boston, MA 02110
info@merclearning.com
www.merclearning.com
800-232-0223

O. Campesato. *Google® Gemini for Python: Coding with Bard.*
ISBN: 978-1-50152-274-1

The publisher recognizes and respects all marks used by companies, manufacturers, and developers as a means to distinguish their products. All brand names and product names mentioned in this book are trademarks or service marks of their respective companies. Any omission or misuse (of any kind) of service marks or trademarks, etc. is not an attempt to infringe on the property of others.

Library of Congress Control Number: 2024930869
242526321   This book is printed on acid-free paper in the United States of America.

Our titles are available for adoption, license, or bulk purchase by institutions, corporations, etc. For additional information, please contact the Customer Service Dept. at 800-232-0223(toll free).

All of our titles are available in digital format at academiccourseware.com and other digital vendors. *Companion files (figures and code listings) for this title are available by contacting info@merclearning.com.* The sole obligation of MERCURY LEARNING AND INFORMATION to the purchaser is to replace the files, based on defective materials or faulty workmanship, but not based on the operation or functionality of the product.

I'd like to dedicate this book to my parents
– may this bring joy and happiness into their lives.

CONTENTS

*P*REFACE

This book starts with an introduction to fundamental aspects of Python programming, which include various data types, number formatting, Unicode and UTF-8 handling, and text manipulation techniques. In addition. you will learn about loops, conditional logic, and reserved words in Python. You will also see how to handle user input, manage exceptions, and work with command-line arguments.

Next, the text transitions to the realm of Generative AI, discussing its distinction from Conversational AI. Popular platforms and models, including Bard and its competitors, are presented to give readers an understanding of the current AI landscape. The book also sheds light on the capabilities of Bard, its strengths, weaknesses, and potential applications. In addition, you will learn how to generate a variety of Python 3 code samples via Bard.

In essence, this book provides a modest bridge between the worlds of Python programming and AI, aiming to equip readers with the knowledge and skills to navigate both domains confidently.

THE TARGET AUDIENCE

This book is intended primarily for people who want to learn both Python and how to use Bard with Python. This book is also intended to reach an international audience of readers with highly diverse backgrounds in various age groups. In addition, this book uses standard English rather than colloquial expressions that might be confusing to those readers. This book provides a comfortable and meaningful learning experience for the intended readers.

DO I NEED TO LEARN THE THEORY PORTIONS OF THIS BOOK?

The answer depends on the extent to which you plan to become involved in working with Bard and Python, perhaps involving LLMs and generative AI. In general, it's probably worthwhile to learn the more theoretical aspects of LLMs that are discussed in this book.

WHAT DO I NEED TO KNOW FOR THIS BOOK?

Although this book is introductory in nature, some knowledge of Python 3.x with certainly be helpful for the code samples. Knowledge of other programming languages (such as Java) can also be helpful because of the exposure to programming concepts and constructs.

DOES THIS BOOK CONTAIN PRODUCTION-LEVEL CODE SAMPLES?

This book contains basic code samples that are written in Python, and their primary purpose is to familiarize you with basic Python to help you understand the Python code generated via Bard. Moreover, clarity has higher priority than writing more compact code that is more difficult to understand (and possibly more prone to bugs). If you decide to use any of the code in this book, you ought to subject that code to the same rigorous analysis as the other parts of your code base.

COMPANION FILES

All the code samples and figures in this book may be obtained by writing to the publisher at *info@merclearning.com*.

If you are primarily interested in machine learning, there are some subfields of machine learning, such as deep learning and reinforcement learning (and deep reinforcement learning) that might appeal to you. Fortunately, there are many resources available, and you can perform an Internet search for those resources. One other point: the aspects of machine learning for you to learn will depend on your career: the needs of a machine learning engineer, data scientist, manager, student, or software developer are all different.

Oswald Campesato
January 2024

## CHAPTER 1

INTRODUCTION TO PYTHON 3

This chapter contains an introduction to Python, with information about useful tools for installing Python modules, basic Python constructs, and how to work with some data types in Python.

The first part of this chapter covers how to install Python, some Python environment variables, and how to use the Python interpreter. You will see Python code samples and also how to save Python code in text files that you can launch from the command line. The second part of this chapter shows you how to work with simple data types, such as numbers, fractions, and strings. The final part of this chapter discusses exceptions and how to use them in Python scripts.

NOTE *The* Python *files in this book are for* Python *3.x.*

TOOLS FOR PYTHON

The Anaconda Python distribution is available for Windows, Linux, and Mac, and it's downloadable here: *http://continuum.io/downloads*

Anaconda is well-suited for modules such as numpy and scipy, and if you are a Windows user, Anaconda appears to be a better alternative than working from the command line.

easy_install and pip

Both easy_install and pip are very easy to use when you need to install Python modules. Whenever you need to install a Python module (and there are many in this book), use either easy_install or pip with the following syntax:

```
easy_install <module-name>
pip install <module-name>
```

NOTE *Python-based modules are easier to install than modules with code written in C because they are usually faster. However, they are more difficult in terms of installation.*

virtualenv

The `virtualenv` tool enables you to create isolated Python environments, and its home page is here: *http://www.virtualenv.org/en/latest/virtualenv.html*

`virtualenv` addresses the problem of preserving the correct dependencies and versions (and indirectly permissions) for different applications. If you are a Python novice, you might not need `virtualenv` right now, but keep this tool in mind.

IPython

Another very good tool is `IPython` (which won a Jolt award), and its home page is here:

http://ipython.org/install.html

Two very nice features of `IPython` are tab expansion and "?," and an example of tab expansion is shown here:

```
$ ipython3
Python 3.9.13 (main, May 24 2022, 21:28:12)
Type 'copyright', 'credits' or 'license' for more information
IPython 8.14.0 -- An enhanced Interactive Python. Type '?' for help.
In [1]:


In [1]: di
%dirs    dict    dir    divmod
```

In the preceding session, if you type the characters `di`, iPython responds with the following line that contains all the functions that start with the letters `di`:

```
%dirs    dict    dir    divmod
```

If you enter a question mark ("?"), `ipython` provides textual assistance, the first part of which is here:

```
IPython -- An enhanced Interactive Python
==========================================

IPython offers a combination of convenient shell
features, special commands and a history mechanism
for both input (command history) and output (results
caching, similar to Mathematica). It is intended to be
a fully compatible replacement for the standard Python
interpreter, while offering vastly improved functionality
and flexibility.
```

The next section shows you how to check whether or not `Python` is installed on your machine, and also where you can download Python.

PYTHON INSTALLATION

Before you download anything, check if you already have Python installed on your machine (which is likely if you have a Macbook or a Linux machine) by typing the following command in a command shell:

```
python -V
```

The output for the Macbook used in this book is here:

```
Python 3.9.1
```

NOTE *Install Python 3.9 (or as close as possible to this version) on your machine so that you will have the same version of* `Python` *that was used to test the* `Python` *files in this book.*

If you need to install `Python` on your machine, navigate to the `Python` home page and select the downloads link or navigate directly to this website:

http://www.python.org/download/

In addition, `PythonWin` is available for Windows, and its home page is here:

http://www.cgl.ucsf.edu/Outreach/pc204/pythonwin.html

Use any text editor that can create, edit, and save `Python` scripts and save them as plain text files (don't use Microsoft Word).

After you have `Python` installed and configured on your machine, you are ready to work with the `Python` scripts in this book.

SETTING THE PATH ENVIRONMENT VARIABLE (WINDOWS ONLY)

The `PATH` environment variable specifies a list of directories that are searched whenever you specify an executable program from the command line. A very good guide to setting up your environment so that the Python executable is always available in every command shell is to follow the instructions here:

http://www.blog.pythonlibrary.org/2011/11/24/python-101-setting-up-python-on-windows/

LAUNCHING PYTHON ON YOUR MACHINE

There are three different ways to launch Python:

- Use the Python Interactive Interpreter.
- Launch Python scripts from the command line.
- Use an IDE.

The next section shows you how to launch the `Python` interpreter from the command line, and later in this chapter you will learn how to launch `Python` scripts from the command line and also about `Python` IDEs.

NOTE

The emphasis in this book is to launch `Python` *files from the command line or to enter code in the* `Python` *interpreter.*

The Python Interactive Interpreter

Launch the `Python` interactive interpreter from the command line by opening a command shell and typing the following command:

```
python
```

You will see the following prompt (or something similar):

```
Python 3.9.1 (v3.9.1:1e5d33e9b9, Dec  7 2020, 12:44:01)
[Clang 12.0.0 (clang-1200.0.32.27)] on darwin
Type "help", "copyright", "credits" or "license" for more
information.
>>>
```

Now type the expression 2 + 7 at the prompt:

```
>>> 2 + 7
Python displays the following result:
9
>>>
```

Press `ctrl-d` to exit the `Python` shell.

You can launch any `Python` script from the command line by preceding it with the word "python." For example, if you have a `Python` script `myscript.py` that contains Python commands, launch the script as follows:

```
python myscript.py
```

As a simple illustration, suppose that the `Python` script `myscript.py` contains the following `Python` code:

```
print('Hello World from Python')
print('2 + 7 = ', 2+7)
```

When you launch the preceding `Python` script, you will see the following output:

```
Hello World from Python
2 + 7 =  9
```

PYTHON IDENTIFIERS

A `Python` identifier is the name of a variable, function, class, module, or other `Python` object, and a valid identifier conforms to the following rules:

- It starts with a letter A to Z or a to z or an underscore (_).
- It includes zero or more letters, underscores, and digits (0 to 9).

NOTE *Python identifiers cannot contain characters such as @, $, and %.*

`Python` is a case-sensitive language, so `Abc` and `abc` different identifiers in Python.

In addition, `Python` has the following naming convention:

- Class names start with an uppercase letter and all other identifiers with a lowercase letter.
- An initial underscore is used for private identifiers.
- Two initial underscores are used for strongly private identifiers.

A `Python` identifier with two initial underscore and two trailing underscore characters indicates a language-defined special name.

LINES, INDENTATION, AND MULTILINES

Unlike other programming languages (such as Java or Objective-C), `Python` uses indentation instead of curly braces for code blocks. Indentation must be consistent in a code block, as shown here:

```
if True:
    print("ABC")
    print("DEF")
else:
    print("ABC")
    print("DEF")
```

Multiline statements in `Python` can terminate with a new line or the back-slash ("\") character, as shown here:

```
total = x1 + \
        x2 + \
        x3
```

Obviously you can place `x1`, `x2`, and `x3` on the same line, so there is no reason to use three separate lines; however, this functionality is available in case you need to add a set of variables that do not fit on a single line.

You can specify multiple statements in one line by using a semicolon (";") to separate each statement, as shown here:

```
a=10; b=5; print(a); print(a+b)
```

The output of the preceding code snippet is here:

```
10
15
```

The use of semi-colons and the continuation character are discouraged in Python.

QUOTATION AND COMMENTS IN PYTHON

Python allows single (`'`), double (`"`) and triple (`'''` or `"""`) quotes for string literals, provided that they match at the beginning and the end of the string. You can use triple quotes for strings that span multiple lines. The following examples are legal Python strings:

```
word = 'word'
line = "This is a sentence."
para = """This is a paragraph. This paragraph contains
more than one sentence."""
```

A string literal that begins with the letter "r" (for "raw") treats everything as a literal character and "escapes" the meaning of meta characters, as shown here:

```
a1 = r'\n'
a2 = r'\r'
a3 = r'\t'
print('a1:',a1,'a2:',a2,'a3:',a3)
```

The output of the preceding code block is here:

```
a1: \n a2: \r a3: \t
```

You can embed a single quote in a pair of double quotes (and vice versa) in order to display a single quote or a double quote. Another way to accomplish the same result is to precede a single or double quote with a backslash ("\") character. The following code block illustrates these techniques:

```
b1 = "'"
b2 = '"'
b3 = '\''
b4 = "\""
print('b1:',b1,'b2:',b2)
print('b3:',b3,'b4:',b4)
```

The output of the preceding code block is here:

```
b1: ' b2: "
b3: ' b4: "
```

A hash sign (#) that is not inside a string literal is the character that indicates the beginning of a comment. Moreover, all characters after the # and up to the physical line end are part of the comment (and ignored by the Python interpreter). Consider the following code block:

```
#!/usr/bin/python
# First comment
print("Hello, Python!")   # second comment
```

This will produce following result:

```
Hello, Python!
```

A comment may be on the same line after a statement or expression:

```
name = "Tom Jones" # This is also comment
```

You can comment multiple lines as follows:

```
# This is comment one
# This is comment two
# This is comment three
```

A blank line in Python is a line containing only white space, a comment, or both.

SAVING YOUR CODE IN A MODULE

Earlier you saw how to launch the Python interpreter from the command line and then enter Python commands. However, that everything that you type in the Python interpreter is only valid for the current session: if you exit the interpreter and then launch the interpreter again, your previous definitions are no longer valid. Fortunately, Python enables you to store code in a text file, as discussed in the next section.

A *module* in Python is a text file that contains Python statements. In the previous section, you saw how the Python interpreter enables you to test code snippets whose definitions are valid for the current session. If you want to retain the code snippets and other definitions, place them in a text file so that you can execute that code outside of the Python interpreter.

The outermost statements in a Python are executed from top to bottom when the module is imported for the first time, which will then set up its variables and functions.

A `Python` module can be run directly from the command line, as shown here:

```
python first.py
```

As an illustration, place the following two statements in a text file called `first.py`:

```
x = 3
print(x)
```

Now type the following command:

```
python first.py
```

The output from the preceding command is 3, which is the same as executing the preceding code from the Python interpreter.

When a `Python` module is run directly, the special variable `__name__` is set to `__main__`. You will often see the following type of code in a Python module:

```
if __name__ == '__main__':
    # do something here
    print('Running directly')
```

The preceding code snippet enables `Python` to determine if a `Python` module was launched from the command line or imported into another Python module.

SOME STANDARD MODULES IN PYTHON

The `Python Standard Library` provides many modules that can simplify your own `Python` scripts. A list of the Standard Library modules is here:

http://www.python.org/doc/

Some of the most important `Python` modules include `cgi`, `math`, `os`, `pickle`, `random`, `re`, `socket`, `sys`, `time`, and `urllib`.

The code samples in this book use the modules `math`, `os`, `random`, `re`, `socket`, `sys`, `time`, and `urllib`. You need to import these modules in order to use them in your code. For example, the following code block shows you how to import four standard Python modules:

```
import datetime
import re
import sys
import time
```

The code samples in this book import one or more of the preceding modules, as well as other `Python` modules.

THE `help()` AND `dir()` FUNCTIONS

An internet search for `Python`-related topics usually returns a number of links with useful information. Alternatively, you can check the official `Python` documentation site: docs.python.org

In addition, `Python` provides the `help()` and `dir()` functions that are accessible from the `Python` interpreter. The `help()` function displays documentation strings, whereas the `dir()` function displays defined symbols.

For example, if you type `help(sys)` you will see documentation for the `sys` module, whereas `dir(sys)` displays a list of the defined symbols.

Type the following command in the `Python` interpreter to display the string-related methods in `Python`:

```
>>> dir(str)
```

The preceding command generates the following output:

```
['__add__', '__class__', '__contains__', '__delattr__',
'__doc__', '__eq__', '__format__', '__ge__',
'__getattribute__', '__getitem__', '__getnewargs__',
'__getslice__', '__gt__', '__hash__', '__init__', '__le__',
'__len__', '__lt__', '__mod__', '__mul__', '__ne__',
'__new__', '__reduce__', '__reduce_ex__', '__repr__',
'__rmod__', '__rmul__', '__setattr__', '__sizeof__',
'__str__', '__subclasshook__', '_formatter_field_name_
split', '_formatter_parser', 'capitalize', 'center',
'count', 'decode', 'encode', 'endswith', 'expandtabs',
'find', 'format', 'index', 'isalnum', 'isalpha', 'isdigit',
'islower', 'isspace', 'istitle', 'isupper', 'join',
'ljust', 'lower', 'lstrip', 'partition', 'replace',
'rfind', 'rindex', 'rjust', 'rpartition', 'rsplit',
'rstrip', 'split', 'splitlines', 'startswith', 'strip',
'swapcase', 'title', 'translate', 'upper', 'zfill']
```

The preceding list gives you a consolidated "dump" of built-in functions (including some that are discussed later in this chapter). Although the `max()` function obviously returns the maximum value of its arguments, the purpose of other functions such as `filter()` or `map()` is not immediately apparent (unless you have used them in other programming languages). In any case, the preceding list provides a starting point for finding out more about various `Python` built-in functions that are not discussed in this chapter.

Note that while `dir()` does not list the names of built-in functions and variables, you can obtain this information from the standard module `__builtin__` that is automatically imported under the name `__builtins__`:

```
>>> dir(__builtins__)
```

The following command shows you how to get more information about a function:

```
help(str.lower)
```

The output from the preceding command is here:

```
Help on method_descriptor:

lower(...)
    S.lower() -> string

    Return a copy of the string S converted to lowercase.
(END)
```

Check the online documentation and also experiment with `help()` and `dir()` when you need additional information about a particular function or module.

COMPILE TIME AND RUNTIME CODE CHECKING

`Python` performs some compile-time checking, but most checks (including type, name, and so forth) are *deferred* until code execution. Consequently, if your `Python` code references a user-defined function that that does not exist, the code will compile successfully. In fact, the code will fail with an exception *only* when the code execution path references the nonexistent function.

As a simple example, consider the following `Python` function `myFunc` that references the nonexistent function called `DoesNotExist`:

```
def myFunc(x):
    if x == 3:
        print(DoesNotExist(x))
    else:
        print('x: ',x)
```

The preceding code will only fail when the `myFunc` function is passed the value 3: Python raises an error when the first print() statement is executed.

In Chapter 2, you will learn how to define and invoke user-defined functions, along with an explanation of the difference between local versus global variables in `Python`.

Now that you understand some basic concepts (such as how to use the Python interpreter) and how to launch your custom `Python` modules, the next section discusses primitive data types in Python.

SIMPLE DATA TYPES IN PYTHON

`Python` supports primitive data types, such as numbers (integers, floating point numbers, and exponential numbers), strings, and dates. `Python` also supports more complex data types, such as lists (or arrays), tuples, and dictionaries, all of which are discussed in Chapter 3. The next several sections discuss some of the Python primitive data types, along with code snippets that show you how to perform various operations on those data types.

WORKING WITH NUMBERS

Python provides arithmetic operations for manipulating numbers a straightforward manner that is similar to other programming languages. The following examples involve arithmetic operations on integers:

```
>>> 2+2
4
>>> 4/3
1
>>> 3*8
24
```

The following example assigns numbers to two variables and computes their product:

```
>>> x = 4
>>> y = 7
>>> x * y
28
```

The following examples demonstrate arithmetic operations involving integers:

```
>>> 2+2
4
>>> 4/3
1
>>> 3*8
24
```

Notice that division ("/") of two integers is actually truncation in which only the integer result is retained. The following example converts a floating point number into exponential form:

```
>>> fnum = 0.00012345689000007
>>> "%.14e"%fnum
'1.23456890000070e-04'
```

You can use the int() function and the float() function to convert strings to numbers:

```
word1 = "123"
word2 = "456.78"
var1 = int(word1)
var2 = float(word2)
print("var1: ",var1," var2: ",var2)
```

The output from the preceding code block is here:

```
var1:   123   var2:   456.78
```

Alternatively, you can use the `eval()` function:

```
word1 = "123"
word2 = "456.78"
var1 = eval(word1)
var2 = eval(word2)
print("var1: ",var1," var2: ",var2)
```

If you attempt to convert a string that is not a valid integer or a floating point number, `Python` raises an exception, so it's advisable to place your code in a `try/except` block (discussed later in this chapter).

Working With Other Bases

Numbers in `Python` are in base 10 (the default), but you can easily convert numbers to other bases. For example, the following code block initializes the variable x with the value `1234`, and then displays that number in base `2`, `8`, and `16`, respectively:

```
>>> x = 1234
>>> bin(x) '0b10011010010'
>>> oct(x) '0o2322'
>>> hex(x) '0x4d2' >>>
```

Use the `format()` function if you wan to suppress the `0b`, `0o`, or `0x` prefixes, as shown here:

```
>>> format(x, 'b') '10011010010'
>>> format(x, 'o') '2322'
>>> format(x, 'x') '4d2'
```

Negative integers are displayed with a negative sign:

```
>>> x = -1234
>>> format(x, 'b') '-10011010010'
>>> format(x, 'x') '-4d2'
```

The `chr()` Function

The `Python` `chr()` function takes a positive integer as a parameter and converts it to its corresponding alphabetic value (if one exists). The letters A through Z have decimal representation of `65` through `91` (which corresponds to hexadecimal `41` through `5b`), and the lowercase letters a through z have decimal representation `97` through `122` (hexadecimal `61` through `7a`).

Here is an example of using the `chr()` function to print uppercase A:

```
>>> x=chr(65)
>>> x
'A'
```

The following code block prints the ASCII values for a range of integers:

```
result = ""
for x in range(65,91):
  print(x, chr(x))
  result = result+chr(x)+' '
print("result: ",result)
```

NOTE   Python 2 *uses* ASCII *strings whereas* Python 3 *uses* UTF-8.

You can represent a range of characters with the following line:

```
for x in range(65,91):
```

However, the following equivalent code snippet is more intuitive:

```
for x in range(ord('A'), ord('Z')):
```

If you want to display the result for lowercase letters, change the preceding range from (65,91) to either of the following statements:

```
for x in range(65,91):
for x in range(ord('a'), ord('z')):
```

The round() **Function in Python**

The Python round() function enables you to round decimal values to the nearest precision:

```
>>> round(1.23, 1)
1.2
>>> round(-3.42,1)
-3.4
```

Formatting Numbers in Python

Python allows you to specify the number of decimal places of precision to use when printing decimal numbers, as shown here:

```
>>> x = 1.23456
>>> format(x, '0.2f')
'1.23'
>>> format(x, '0.3f')
'1.235'
>>> 'value is {:0.3f}'.format(x) 'value is 1.235'
>>> from decimal import Decimal
>>> a = Decimal('4.2')
>>> b = Decimal('2.1')
>>> a + b
Decimal('6.3')
>>> print(a + b)
6.3
>>> (a + b) == Decimal('6.3')
True
```

```
>>> x = 1234.56789
>>> # Two decimal places of accuracy
>>> format(x, '0.2f')
'1234.57'
>>> # Right justified in 10 chars, one-digit accuracy
>>> format(x, '>10.1f')
'  1234.6'
>>> # Left justified
>>> format(x, '<10.1f') '1234.6  '
>>> # Centered
>>> format(x, '^10.1f') '  1234.6  '
>>> # Inclusion of thousands separator
>>> format(x, ',')
'1,234.56789'
>>> format(x, '0,.1f')
'1,234.6'
```

WORKING WITH FRACTIONS

Python supports the Fraction() function (which is define in the fractions module) that accepts two integers that represent the numerator and the denominator (which must be nonzero) of a fraction. Several example of defining and manipulating fractions in Python are shown here:

```
>>> from fractions import Fraction
>>> a = Fraction(5, 4)
>>> b = Fraction(7, 16)
>>> print(a + b)
27/16
>>> print(a * b) 35/64
>>> # Getting numerator/denominator
>>> c = a * b
>>> c.numerator
35
>>> c.denominator 64
>>> # Converting to a float >>> float(c)
0.546875
>>> # Limiting the denominator of a value
>>> print(c.limit_denominator(8))
4
>>> # Converting a float to a fraction >>> x = 3.75
>>> y = Fraction(*x.as_integer_ratio())
>>> y
Fraction(15, 4)
```

Before delving into Python code samples that work with strings, the next section briefly discusses Unicode and UTF-8, both of which are character encodings.

UNICODE AND UTF-8

A Unicode string consists of a sequence of numbers that are between 0 and 0x10ffff, where each number represents a group of bytes. An encoding is the manner in which a Unicode string is translated into a sequence of bytes.

Among the various encodings, UTF-8 ("Unicode transformation format") is perhaps the most common, and it's also the default encoding for many systems. The digit 8 in UTF-8 indicates that the encoding uses 8-bit numbers, whereas UTF-16 uses 16-bit numbers (but this encoding is less common).

The ASCII character set is a subset of UTF-8, so a valid ASCII string can be read as a UTF-8 string without any re-encoding required. In addition, a Unicode string can be converted into a UTF-8 string.

WORKING WITH UNICODE

Python supports Unicode, which means that you can render characters in different languages. Unicode data can be stored and manipulated in the same way as strings. Create a Unicode string by prepending the letter 'u', as shown here:

```
>>> u'Hello from Python!'
u'Hello from Python!'
```

Special characters can be included in a string by specifying their Unicode value. For example, the following Unicode string embeds a space (which has the Unicode value 0x0020) in a string:

```
>>> u'Hello\u0020from Python!'
u'Hello from Python!'
```

Listing 1.1 displays the contents of unicode1.py that illustrates how to display a string of characters in Japanese and another string of characters in Chinese (Mandarin).

LISTING 1.1: unicode1.py

```
chinese1 = u'\u5c07\u63a2\u8a0e HTML5 \u53ca\u5176\u4ed6'
hiragana = u'D3 \u306F \u304B\u3063\u3053\u3043\u3043 \u3067\u3059!'

print('Chinese:',chinese1)
print('Hiragana:',hiragana)
```

The output of Listing 1.2 is here:

```
Chinese: 將探討 HTML5 及其他
Hiragana: D3 は かっこいい です!
```

The next portion of this chapter shows you how to "slice and dice" text strings with built-in Python functions.

WORKING WITH STRINGS

You can concatenate two strings using the '+' operator. The following example prints a string and then concatenates two single-letter strings:

```
>>> 'abc'
'abc'
```

```
>>> 'a' + 'b'
'ab'
```

You can use "+" or "*" to concatenate identical strings, as shown here:

```
>>> 'a' + 'a' + 'a'
'aaa'
>>> 'a' * 3
'aaa'
```

You can assign strings to variables and print them using the `print()` command:

```
>>> print('abc')
abc
>>> x = 'abc'
>>> print(x)
abc
>>> y = 'def'
>>> print(x + y)
abcdef
```

You can "unpack" the letters of a string and assign them to variables, as shown here:

```
>>> str = "World"
>>> x1,x2,x3,x4,x5 = str
>>> x1
'W'
>>> x2
'o'
>>> x3
'r'
>>> x4
'l'
>>> x5
'd'
```

The preceding code snippets shows you how easy it is to extract the letters in a text string, and in Chapter 3 you will learn how to "unpack" other `Python` data structures.

You can extract substrings of a string as shown in the following examples:

```
>>> x = "abcdef"
>>> x[0]
'a'
>>> x[-1]
'f'
>>> x[1:3]
'bc'
>>> x[0:2] + x[5:]
'abf'
```

However, you will cause an error if you attempt to "subtract" two strings, as you probably expect:

```
>>> 'a' - 'b'
Traceback (most recent call last):
  File "<stdin>", line 1, in <module>
TypeError: unsupported operand type(s) for -: 'str' and 'str'
```

The `try/except` construct in `Python` (discussed later in this chapter) enables you to handle the preceding type of exception more gracefully.

Comparing Strings

You can use the methods `lower()` and `upper()` to convert a string to lowercase and uppercase, respectively, as shown here:

```
>>> 'Python'.lower()
'python'
>>> 'Python'.upper()
'PYTHON'
>>>
```

The methods `lower()` and `upper()` are useful for performing a case insensitive comparison of two ASCII strings. Listing 1.2 displays the contents of compare.py that uses the `lower()` function in order to compare two ASCII strings.

LISTING 1.2: compare.py

```
x = 'Abc'
y = 'abc'

if(x == y):
  print('x and y: identical')
elif (x.lower() == y.lower()):
  print('x and y: case insensitive match')
else:
  print('x and y: different')
```

Since x contains mixed case letters and y contains lowercase letters, Listing 1.2 displays the following output:

```
x and y: different
```

Formatting Strings in Python

`Python` provides the functions `string.lstring()`, `string.rstring()`, and `string.center()` for positioning a text string so that it is left-justified, right-justified, and centered, respectively. As you saw in a previous section, `Python` also provides the `format()` method for advanced interpolation features.

Now enter the following commands in the Python interpreter:

```
import string

str1 = 'this is a string'
print(string.ljust(str1, 10))
print(string.rjust(str1, 40))
print(string.center(str1,40))
```

The output is shown here:

```
this is a string
                        this is a string
            this is a string
```

The next portion of this chapter shows you how to "slice and dice" text strings with built-in Python functions.

SLICING AND SPLICING STRINGS

Python enables you to extract substrings of a string (called "slicing") using array notation. Slice notation is start:stop:step, where the start, stop, and step values are integers that specify the start value, end value, and the increment value. The interesting part about slicing in Python is that you can use the value -1, which operates from the right side of a string instead of the left side of a string.

Some examples of slicing a string are here:

```
text1 = "this is a string"
print('First 7 characters:',text1[0:7])
print('Characters 2-4:',text1[2:4])
print('Right-most character:',text1[-1])
print('Right-most 2 characters:',text1[-3:-1])
```

The output from the preceding code block is here:

```
First 7 characters: this is
Characters 2-4: is
Right-most character: g
Right-most 2 characters: in
```

Later in this chapter you will see how to insert a string in the middle of another string.

Testing for Digits and Alphabetic Characters

Python enables you to examine each character in a string and then test whether that character is a bona fide digit or an alphabetic character. This section provides simple examples of regular expressions.

Listing 1.3 displays the contents of char_types.py that illustrates how to determine if a string contains digits or characters. In case you are unfamiliar with the conditional "if" statement in Listing 1.3, more detailed information is available in Chapter 2.

LISTING 1.3: char_types.py

```
str1 = "4"
str2 = "4234"
str3 = "b"
str4 = "abc"
str5 = "a1b2c3"

if(str1.isdigit()):
  print("this is a digit:",str1)

if(str2.isdigit()):
  print("this is a digit:",str2)

if(str3.isalpha()):
  print("this is alphabetic:",str3)

if(str4.isalpha()):
  print("this is alphabetic:",str4)

if(not str5.isalpha()):
  print("this is not pure alphabetic:",str5)

print("capitalized first letter:",str5.title())
```

Listing 1.3 initializes some variables, followed by 2 conditional tests that check whether or not `str1` and `str2` are digits using the `isdigit()` function. The next portion of Listing 1.3 checks if `str3, str4,` and `str5` are alphabetic strings using the `isalpha()` function. The output of Listing 1.3 is here:

```
this is a digit: 4
this is a digit: 4234
this is alphabetic: b
this is alphabetic: abc
this is not pure alphabetic: a1b2c3
capitalized first letter: A1B2C3
```

SEARCH AND REPLACE A STRING IN OTHER STRINGS

Python provides methods for searching and also for replacing a string in a second text string. Listing 1.4 displays the contents of `find_pos1.py` that shows you how to use the find function to search for the occurrence of one string in another string.

LISTING 1.4: find_pos1.py

```
item1 = 'abc'
item2 = 'Abc'
text = 'This is a text string with abc'
```

```
pos1 = text.find(item1)
pos2 = text.find(item2)

print('pos1=',pos1)
print('pos2=',pos2)
```

Listing 1.4 initializes the variables item1, item2, and text, and then searches for the index of the contents of item1 and item2 in the string text. The Python find() function returns the column number where the first successful match occurs; otherwise, the find() function returns a –1 if a match is unsuccessful.

The output from launching Listing 1.4 is here:

```
pos1= 27
pos2= -1
```

In addition to the find() method, you can use the in operator when you want to test for the presence of an element, as shown here:

```
>>> lst = [1,2,3]
>>> 1 in lst
True
```

Listing 1.5 displays the contents of replace1.py that shows you how to replace one string with another string.

LISTING 1.5: replace1.py

```
text = 'This is a text string with abc'
print('text:',text)
text = text.replace('is a', 'was a')
print('text:',text)
```

Listing 1.5 starts by initializing the variable text and then printing its contents. The next portion of Listing 1.5 replaces the occurrence of "is a" with "was a" in the string text, and then prints the modified string. The output from launching Listing 1.5 is here:

```
text: This is a text string with abc
text: This was a text string with abc
```

REMOVE LEADING AND TRAILING CHARACTERS

Python provides the functions strip(), lstrip(), and rstrip() to remove characters in a text string. Listing 1.6 displays the contents of remove1.py that shows you how to search for a string.

LISTING 1.6: remove1.py

```
text = '   leading and trailing white space   '
print('text1:', 'x',text,'y')
```

```
text = text.lstrip()
print('text2:','x',text,'y')

text = text.rstrip()
print('text3:','x',text,'y')
```

Listing 1.6 starts by concatenating the letter x and the contents of the variable text, and then printing the result. The second part of Listing 1.6 removes the leading white spaces in the string text and then appends the result to the letter x. The third part of Listing 1.6 removes the trailing white spaces in the string text (note that the leading white spaces have already been removed) and then appends the result to the letter x.

The output from launching Listing 1.6 is here:

```
text1: x    leading and trailing white space    y
text2: x leading and trailing white space    y
text3: x leading and trailing white space y
```

If you want to remove extra white spaces inside a text string, use the replace() function as discussed in the previous section. The following example illustrates how this can be accomplished, which also contains the re module as an example of regular expressions in Python:

```
import re
text = 'a    b'
a = text.replace(' ', '')
b = re.sub('\s+', ' ', text)

print(a)
print(b)
```

The result is here:

```
ab
a b
```

Chapter 2 shows you how to use the join() function in order to remove extra white spaces in a text string.

PRINTING TEXT WITHOUT NEWLINE CHARACTERS

If you need to suppress white space and a newline between objects output with multiple print() statements, you can use concatenation or the write() function.

The first technique is to concatenate the string representations of each object using the str() function prior to printing the result. For example, run the following statement in Python:

```
x = str(9)+str(0xff)+str(-3.1)
print('x: ',x)
```

The output is shown here:

```
x:   9255-3.1
```

The preceding line contains the concatenation of the numbers 9 and 255 (which is the decimal value of the hexadecimal number 0xff) and -3.1.

Incidentally, you can use the str() function with modules and user-defined classes. An example involving the Python built-in module sys is here:

```
>>> import sys
>>> print(str(sys))
<module 'sys' (built-in)>
```

The following code snippet illustrates how to use the write() function to display a string:

```
import sys
write = sys.stdout.write
write('123')
write('123456789')
```

The output is here:

```
123123456789
```

TEXT ALIGNMENT

Python provides the methods ljust(), rjust(), and center() for aligning text. The ljust() and rjust() functions left justify and right justify a text string, respectively, whereas the center() function will center a string. An example is shown in the following code block:

```
text = 'Hello World'
text.ljust(20)
'Hello World '
>>> text.rjust(20)
'         Hello World'
>>> text.center(20)
'    Hello World     '
```

You can use the Python format() function to align text. Use the <, >, or ^ characters, along with a desired width, in order to right justify, left justify, and center the text, respectively. The following examples illustrate how you can specify text justification:

```
>>> format(text, '>20')
'         Hello World'
>>>
>>> format(text, '<20')
'Hello World         '
```

```
>>>
>>> format(text, '^20')
'     Hello World     '
>>>
```

WORKING WITH DATES

Python provides a rich set of date-related functions. Listing 1.7 displays the contents of the Python script date_time2.py that displays various date-related values, such as the current date and time; the day of the week, month, and year; and the time in seconds since the epoch.

LISTING 1.7: date_time2.py

```python
import time
import datetime

print("Time in seconds since the epoch: %s" %time.time())
print("Current date and time: " , datetime.datetime.now())
print("Or like this: " ,datetime.datetime.now().
strftime("%y-%m-%d-%H-%M"))

print("Current year: ", datetime.date.today().
strftime("%Y"))
print("Month of year: ", datetime.date.today().
strftime("%B"))
print("Week number of the year: ", datetime.date.today().
strftime("%W"))
print("Weekday of the week: ", datetime.date.today().
strftime("%w"))
print("Day of year: ", datetime.date.today().
strftime("%j"))
print("Day of the month : ", datetime.date.today().
strftime("%d"))
print("Day of week: ", datetime.date.today().
strftime("%A"))
```

Listing 1.8 displays the output generated by running the code in Listing 1.7.

LISTING 1.8 datetime2.out

```
Time in seconds since the epoch: 1375144195.66
Current date and time:  2013-07-29 17:29:55.664164
Or like this:  13-07-29-17-29
Current year:  2013
Month of year:  July
Week number of the year:  30
Weekday of the week:  1
Day of year:  210
Day of the month :  29
Day of week:  Monday
```

`Python` also enables you to perform arithmetic calculates with date-related values, as shown in the following code block:

```
>>> from datetime import timedelta
>>> a = timedelta(days=2, hours=6)
>>> b = timedelta(hours=4.5)
>>> c = a + b
>>> c.days
2
>>> c.seconds
37800
>>> c.seconds / 3600
10.5
>>> c.total_seconds() / 3600
58.5
```

Converting Strings to Dates

Listing 1.9 displays the contents of `string2date.py` that illustrates how to convert a string to a date, and also how to calculate the difference between two dates.

LISTING 1.9: string2date.py

```
from datetime import datetime

text = '2024-08-13'
y = datetime.strptime(text, '%Y-%m-%d')
z = datetime.now()
diff = z - y
print('Date difference:',diff)
```

The output from Listing 1.9 is shown here:

```
Date difference: -210 days, 18:58:40.197130
```

EXCEPTION HANDLING IN PYTHON

Unlike `JavaScript` you cannot add a number and a string in `Python`. However, you can detect an illegal operation using the `try/except` construct in `Python`, which is similar to the `try/catch` construct in languages such as `JavaScript` and `Java`.

An example of a `try/except` block is here:

```
try:
  x = 4
  y = 'abc'
  z = x + y
except:
  print 'cannot add incompatible types:', x, y
```

When you run the preceding code in Python, the `print()` statement in the `except` code block is executed because the variables x and y have incompatible types.

Earlier in the chapter you also saw that subtracting two strings throws an exception:

```
>>> 'a' - 'b'
Traceback (most recent call last):
  File "<stdin>", line 1, in <module>
TypeError: unsupported operand type(s) for -: 'str' and 'str'
```

A simple way to handle this situation is to use a `try/except` block:

```
>>> try:
...   print('a' - 'b')
... except TypeError:
...   print('TypeError exception while trying to subtract two strings')
... except:
...   print('Exception while trying to subtract two strings')
...
```

The output from the preceding code block is here:

```
TypeError exception while trying to subtract two strings
```

As you can see, the preceding code block specifies the finer-grained exception called `TypeError`, followed by a generic `except` code block to handle all other exceptions that might occur during the execution of your Python code. This style is similar to the exception handling in Java code.

Listing 1.10 displays the contents of `exception1.py` that illustrates how to handle various types of exceptions.

LISTING 1.10: exception1.py

```
import sys

try:
    f = open('myfile.txt')
    s = f.readline()
    i = int(s.strip())
except IOError as err:
    print("I/O error: {0}".format(err))
except ValueError:
    print("Could not convert data to an integer.")
except:
    print("Unexpected error:", sys.exc_info()[0])
    raise
```

Listing 1.10 contains a `try` block followed by three `except` statements. If an error occurs in the `try` block, the first `except` statement is compared with the type of exception that occurred. If there is a match, then the subsequent print() statement is executed, and the program terminates. If not, a similar test is performed with the second `except` statement. If neither `except` statement matches the exception, the third `except` statement handles the exception, which involves printing a message and then "raising" an exception. Note that you can also specify multiple exception types in a single statement, as shown here:

```
except (NameError, RuntimeError, TypeError):
    print('One of three error types occurred')
```

The preceding code block is more compact, but you do not know which of the three error types occurred. `Python` allows you to define custom exceptions, but this topic is beyond the scope of this book.

HANDLING USER INPUT

`Python` enables you to read user input from the command line via the `input()` function or the `raw_input()` function. Typically you assign user input to a variable, which will contain all characters that users enter from the keyboard. User input terminates when users press the `<return>` key (which is included with the input characters). Listing 1.11 displays the contents of `user_input1.py` that prompts users for their name and then uses interpolation to display a response.

LISTING 1.11: user_input1.py

```
userInput = input("Enter your name: ")
print ("Hello %s, my name is Python" % userInput)
```

The output of Listing 1.11 is here (assume that the user entered the word "Dave"):

```
Hello Dave, my name is Python
```

The `print()` statement in Listing 1.11 uses string interpolation via `%s`, which substitutes the value of the variable after the `%` symbol. This functionality is obviously useful when you want to specify something that is determined at run-time.

User input can cause exceptions (depending on the operations that your code performs), so it's important to include exception-handling code.

Listing 1.12 displays the contents of `user_input2.py` that prompts users for a string and attempts to convert the string to a number in a `try/except` block.

LISTING 1.12: user_input2.py

```
userInput = input("Enter something: ")

try:
  x = 0 + eval(userInput)
```

```
    print('you entered the number:',userInput)
except:
    print(userInput,'is a string')
```

Listing 1.12 adds the number 0 to the result of converting a user's input to a number. If the conversion was successful, a message with the user's input is displayed. If the conversion failed, the `except` code block consists of a `print` statement that displays a message.

_____
NOTE *This code sample uses the `eval()` function, which should be avoided so that your code does not evaluate arbitrary (and possibly destructive) commands.*
_____

Listing 1.13 displays the contents of `user_input3.py` that prompts users for two numbers and attempts to compute their sum in a pair of `try/except` blocks.

LISTING 1.13: user_input3.py

```
sum = 0

msg = 'Enter a number:'
val1 = input(msg)

try:
   sum = sum + eval(val1)
except:
   print(val1,'is a string')

msg = 'Enter a number:'
val2 = input(msg)

try:
   sum = sum + eval(val2)
except:
   print(val2,'is a string')

print('The sum of',val1,'and',val2,'is',sum)
```

Listing 1.13 contains two `try` blocks, each of which is followed by an `except` statement. The first `try` block attempts to add the first user-supplied number to the variable `sum`, and the second `try` block attempts to add the second user-supplied number to the previously entered number. An error message occurs if either input string is not a valid number; if both are valid numbers, a message is displayed containing the input numbers and their sum. Be sure to read the caveat regarding the `eval()` function that is mentioned earlier in this chapter.

COMMAND-LINE ARGUMENTS

`Python` provides a `getopt` module to parse command-line options and arguments, and the `Python` `sys` module provides access to any command-line arguments via the `sys.argv`. This serves two purposes:

1. `sys.argv` is the list of command-line arguments.
2. `len(sys.argv)` is the number of command-line arguments.

Here `sys.argv[0]` is the program name, so if the `Python` program is called `test.py`, it matches the value of `sys.argv[0]`.

Now you can provide input values for a `Python` program on the command line instead of providing input values by prompting users for their input.

As an example, consider the script `test.py` shown here:

```
#!/usr/bin/python
import sys
print('Number of arguments:',len(sys.argv),'arguments')
print('Argument List:', str(sys.argv))
```

Now run above script as follows:

```
python test.py arg1 arg2 arg3
```

This will produce following result:

```
Number of arguments: 4 arguments.
Argument List: ['test.py', 'arg1', 'arg2', 'arg3']
```

The ability to specify input values from the command line provides useful functionality. For example, suppose that you have a custom Python class that contains the methods `add` and `subtract` to add and subtract a pair of numbers.

You can use command-line arguments in order to specify which method to execute on a pair of numbers, as shown here:

```
python MyClass add 3 5
python MyClass subtract 3 5
```

This functionality is very useful because you can programmatically execute different methods in a Python class, which means that you can write unit tests for your code as well. Search online for articles that explain how to create custom Python classes.

Listing 1.14 displays the contents of `hello.py` that shows you how to use `sys.argv` to check the number of command line parameters.

LISTING 1.14: hello.py

```
import sys

def main():
  if len(sys.argv) >= 2:
    name = sys.argv[1]
  else:
    name = 'World'
  print('Hello', name)
```

```
# Standard boilerplate to invoke the main() function
if __name__ == '__main__':
   main()
```

Listing 1.14 defines the `main()` function that checks the number of command-line parameters: if this value is at least 2, then the variable `name` is assigned the value of the second parameter (the first parameter is `hello.py`), otherwise `name` is assigned the value `Hello`. The `print()` statement then prints the value of the variable `name`.

The final portion of Listing 1.14 uses conditional logic to determine whether or not to execute the `main()` function.

SUMMARY

This chapter showed you how to work with numbers and perform arithmetic operations on numbers, and then you learned how to work with strings and use string operations. You also learned how to use the try/except construct to handle exceptions that might occur in your `Python` code. The next chapter shows you how to work with conditional statements, loops, and user-defined functions in `Python`.

CONDITIONAL LOGIC, LOOPS, AND FUNCTIONS

This chapter introduces you to various ways to perform conditional logic in Python, as well as control structures and user-defined functions in Python. Virtually every Python program that performs useful calculations requires some type of conditional logic or control structure (or both). Although the syntax for these Python features is slightly different from other languages, the functionality will be familiar to you.

The first part of this chapter contains code samples that illustrate how to handle if-else conditional logic in Python, as well as if-elsif-else statements. The second part of this chapter discusses loops and while statements in Python. This section contains an assortment of examples (comparing strings, computing numbers raised to different exponents, and so forth) that illustrate various ways that you can use loops and while statements in Python.

The third part of this chapter contains examples that involve nested loops and recursion. The final part of this chapter introduces you to user-defined Python functions.

PRECEDENCE OF OPERATORS IN PYTHON

When you have an expression involving numbers, you might remember that multiplication ("*") and division ("/") have higher precedence than addition ("+") or subtraction ("–"). Exponentiation has even higher precedence than these four arithmetic operators.

However, instead of relying on precedence rules, it's simpler (as well as safer) to use parentheses. For example, (x/y)+10 is clearer than x/y+10, even though they are equivalent expressions.

As another example, the following two arithmetic expressions are equivalent, but the second is less error prone than the first:

```
x/y+3*z/8+x*y/z-3*x
(x/y)+(3*z)/8+(x*y)/z-(3*x)
```

In any case, the following website contains precedence rules for operators in `Python`:

http://www.mathcs.emory.edu/~valerie/courses/fall10/155/resources/ op_precedence.html

PYTHON RESERVED WORDS

Every programming language has a set of reserved words, which is a set of words that cannot be used as identifiers, and `Python` is no exception. The Python reserved words are: `and`, `exec`, `not`, `assert`, `finally`, `or`, `break`, `for`, `pass`, `class`, `from`, `print`, `continue`, `global`, `raise`, `def`, `if`, `return`, `del`, `import`, `try`, `elif`, `in`, `while`, `else`, `is`, `with`, `except`, `lambda`, and `yield`.

If you inadvertently use a reserved word as a variable, you will see an "invalid syntax" error message instead of a "reserved word" error message. For example, suppose you create a Python script `test1.py` with the following code:

```
break = 2
print('break =', break)
```

If you run the preceding Python code you will see the following output:

```
  File "test1.py", line 2
    break = 2
          ^
SyntaxError: invalid syntax
```

However, a quick inspection of the `Python` code reveals the fact that you are attempting to use the reserved word `break` as a variable.

WORKING WITH LOOPS IN PYTHON

`Python` supports `for` loops, `while` loops, and `range()` statements. The following subsections illustrate how you can use each of these constructs.

Python `for` Loops

`Python` supports the `for` loop whose syntax is slightly different from other languages (such as JavaScript and Java). The following code block shows you how to use a `for` loop in `Python` in order to iterate through the elements in a list:

```
>>> x = ['a', 'b', 'c']
>>> for w in x:
...     print(w)
...
a
b
c
```

The preceding code snippet prints three letters on three separate lines. You can force the output to be displayed on the same line (which will "wrap" if you specify a large enough number of characters) by appending a comma "," in the print statement, as shown here:

```
>>> x = ['a', 'b', 'c']
>>> for w in x:
...     print(w, end=' ')
...
a b c
```

You can use this type of code when you want to display the contents of a text file in a single line instead of multiple lines.

Python also provides the built-in reversed() function that reverses the direction of the loop, as shown here:

```
>>> a = [1, 2, 3, 4, 5]
>>> for x in reversed(a):
... print(x)
5
4
3
2
1
```

Note that reversed iteration only works if the size of the current object can be determined or if the object implements a __reversed__() special method.

A for **Loop with** try/except **in Python**

Listing 2.1 displays the contents of StringToNums.py that illustrates how to calculate the sum of a set of integers that have been converted from strings.

LISTING 2.1: StringToNums.py

```
line = '1 2 3 4 10e abc'
sum  = 0
invalidStr = ""

print('String of numbers:',line)

for str in line.split(" "):
  try:
    sum = sum + eval(str)
  except:
    invalidStr = invalidStr + str + ' '

print('sum:', sum)
if(invalidStr != ""):
  print('Invalid strings:',invalidStr)
else:
  print('All substrings are valid numbers')
```

Listing 2.1 initializes the variables `line`, `sum`, and `invalidStr`, and then displays the contents of line. The next portion of Listing 2.1 splits the contents of `line` into words, and then uses a `try` block in order to add the numeric value of each word to the variable sum. If an exception occurs, the contents of the current `str` is appended to the variable `invalidStr`.

When the loop has finished execution, Listing 2.1 displays the sum of the numeric words, followed by the list of words that are not numbers. The output from Listing 2.1 is here:

```
String of numbers: 1 2 3 4 10e abc
sum: 10
Invalid strings: 10e abc
```

Numeric Exponents in Python

Listing 2.2 displays the contents of `Nth_exponent.py` that illustrates how to calculate intermediate powers of a set of integers.

LISTING 2.2: Nth_exponent.py

```
maxPower = 4
maxCount = 4

def pwr(num):
  prod = 1
  for n in range(1,maxPower+1):
    prod = prod*num
    print(num,'to the power',n, 'equals',prod)
  print('-----------')

for num in range(1,maxCount+1):
  pwr(num)
```

Listing 2.2 contains a function called `pwr()` that accepts a numeric value. This function contains a loop that prints the value of that number raised to the power n, where n ranges between 1 and `maxPower+1`.

The second part of Listing 2.2 contains a `for` loop that invokes the function `pwr()` with the numbers between 1 and `maxPower+1`. The output from Listing 2.2 is here:

```
1 to the power 1 equals 1
1 to the power 2 equals 1
1 to the power 3 equals 1
1 to the power 4 equals 1
-----------
2 to the power 1 equals 2
2 to the power 2 equals 4
2 to the power 3 equals 8
2 to the power 4 equals 16
-----------
```

```
3 to the power 1 equals 3
3 to the power 2 equals 9
3 to the power 3 equals 27
3 to the power 4 equals 81
-----------
4 to the power 1 equals 4
4 to the power 2 equals 16
4 to the power 3 equals 64
4 to the power 4 equals 256
-----------
```

NESTED LOOPS

Listing 2.3 displays the contents of `Triangular1.py` that illustrates how to print a row of consecutive integers (starting from 1), where the length of each row is one greater than the previous row.

LISTING 2.3: Triangular1.py

```
max = 8
for x in range(1,max+1):
  for y in range(1,x+1):
    print(y, '', end='')
  print()
```

Listing 2.3 initializes the variable `max` with the value 8, followed by an outer `for` loop whose loop variable `x` ranges from 1 to `max+1`. The inner loop has a loop variable `y` that ranges from 1 to `x+1`, and the inner loop prints the value of `y`. The output of Listing 2.4 is here:

```
1
1 2
1 2 3
1 2 3 4
1 2 3 4 5
1 2 3 4 5 6
1 2 3 4 5 6 7
1 2 3 4 5 6 7 8
```

THE split() FUNCTION WITH for LOOPS

`Python` supports various useful string-related functions, including the `split()` function and the `join()` function. The `split()` function is useful when you want to tokenize ("split") a line of text into words and then use a `for` loop to iterate through those words and process them accordingly.

The `join()` function does the opposite of `split()`: it "joins" two or more words into a single line. You can easily remove extra spaces in a sentence by using the `split()` function and then invoking the `join()` function, thereby creating a line of text with one white space between any two words.

USING THE split() FUNCTION TO COMPARE WORDS

Listing 2.4 displays the contents of Compare2.py that illustrates how to use the split function to compare each word in a text string with another word.

LISTING 2.4: Compare2.py

```
x = 'This is a string that contains abc and Abc'
y = 'abc'
identical = 0
casematch = 0

for w in x.split():
  if(w == y):
    identical = identical + 1
  elif (w.lower() == y.lower()):
    casematch = casematch + 1

if(identical > 0):
 print('found identical matches:', identical)

if(casematch > 0):
 print('found case matches:', casematch)

if(casematch == 0 and identical == 0):
 print('no matches found')
```

Listing 2.4 uses the split() function in order to compare each word in the string x with the word abc. If there is an exact match, the variable identical is incremented. If a match does not occur, a case-insensitive match of the current word is performed with the string abc, and the variable casematch is incremented if the match is successful.

The output from Listing 2.5 is here:

```
found identical matches: 1
found case matches: 1
```

USING THE split() FUNCTION TO PRINT JUSTIFIED TEXT

Listing 2.5 displays the contents of FixedColumnCount.py that illustrates how to print a set of words from a text string as justified text using a fixed number of columns.

LISTING 2.5: FixedColumnCount1.py

```
import string

wordCount = 0
str1 = 'this is a string with a set of words in it'

print('Left-justified strings:')
print('----------------------')
```

```
for w in str1.split():
   print('%-10s' % w)
   wordCount = wordCount + 1
   if(wordCount % 2 == 0):
      print("")
print("\n")

print('Right-justified strings:')
print('-----------------------')

wordCount = 0
for w in str1.split():
   print('%10s' % w)
   wordCount = wordCount + 1
   if(wordCount % 2 == 0):
      print()
```

Listing 2.5 initializes the variables wordCount and str1, followed by two for loops. The first for loop prints the words in str1 in left-justified format, and the second for loop prints the words in str1 in right-justified format. In both loops, a linefeed is printed after a pair of consecutive words is printed, which occurs whenever the variable wordCount is even. The output from Listing 2.5 is here:

```
Left-justified strings:
-----------------------
this      is
a         string
with      a
set       of
words     in
it
```

```
Right-justified strings:
-----------------------
       this        is
          a    string
       with         a
        set        of
      words        in
         it
```

USING THE split() FUNCTION TO PRINT FIXED-WIDTH TEXT

Listing 2.6 displays the contents of FixedColumnWidth1.py that illustrates how to print a text string in a column of fixed width.

LISTING 2.6: FixedColumnWidth1.py

```
import string

left = 0
right = 0
columnWidth = 8
```

```
str1 = 'this is a string with a set of words in it and it
will be split into a fixed column width'
strLen = len(str1)

print('Left-justified column:')
print('----------------------')
rowCount = int(strLen/columnWidth)

for i in range(0,rowCount):
    left  = i*columnWidth
    right = (i+1)*columnWidth-1
    word  = str1[left:right]
    print("%-10s" % word)

# check for a 'partial row'
if(rowCount*columnWidth < strLen):
    left  = rowCount*columnWidth-1;
    right = strLen
    word  = str1[left:right]
    print("%-10s" % word)
```

Listing 2.6 initializes the integer variable columnWidth and the string variable str1. The variable strLen is the length of str1, and rowCount is strLen divided by columnWidth.

The next part of Listing 2.6 contains a loop that prints rowCount rows of characters, where each row contains columnWidth characters. The final portion of Listing 2.6 prints any "leftover" characters that comprise a partial row.

The newspaper-style output (but without any partial whitespace formatting) from Listing 2.6 is here:

```
Left-justified column:
----------------------
this is
a strin
 with a
set of
ords in
it and
t will
e split
into a
ixed co
umn wid
th
```

USING THE split() FUNCTION TO COMPARE TEXT STRINGS

Listing 2.7 displays the contents of CompareStrings1.py that illustrates how to determine whether or not the words in one text string are also words in a second text string.

LISTING 2.7: CompareStrings1.py

```
text1 = 'a b c d'
text2 = 'a b c e d'

if(text2.find(text1) >= 0):
  print('text1 is a substring of text2')
else:
  print('text1 is not a substring of text2')

subStr = True
for w in text1.split():
  if(text2.find(w) == -1):
    subStr = False
    break

if(subStr == True):
  print('Every word in text1 is a word in text2')
else:
  print('Not every word in text1 is a word in text2')
```

Listing 2.7 initializes the string variables `text1` and `text2` and uses conditional logic to determine whether or not `text1` is a substring of `text2` (and then prints a suitable message).

The next part of Listing 2.7 is a loop that iterates through the words in the string `text1` and checks if each of those words is also a word in the string `text2`. If a nonmatch occurs, the variable `subStr` is set to False, followed by the break statement that causes an early exit from the loop. The final portion of Listing 2.7 prints the appropriate message based on the value of `subStr`. The output from Listing 2.7 is here:

```
text1 is not a substring of text2
Every word in text1 is a word in text2
```

USING THE `split()` FUNCTION TO DISPLAY CHARACTERS IN A STRING

Listing 2.8 displays the contents of `StringChars1.py` that illustrates how to print the characters in a text string.

LISTING 2.8: StringChars1.py

```
text = 'abcdef'
for ch in text:
    print('char:',ch,'ord value:',ord(ch))
print
```

Listing 2.8 is straightforward: a `for` loop iterates through the characters in the string `text` and then prints the character and its `ord` value. The output from Listing 2.8 is here:

```
('char:', 'a', 'ord value:', 97)
('char:', 'b', 'ord value:', 98)
('char:', 'c', 'ord value:', 99)
('char:', 'd', 'ord value:', 100)
('char:', 'e', 'ord value:', 101)
('char:', 'f', 'ord value:', 102)
```

THE `join()` FUNCTION

Another way to remove extraneous spaces is to use the `join()` function, as shown here:

```
text1 = '   there are     extra    spaces   '
print('text1:',text1)

text2 = ' '.join(text1.split())
print('text2:',text2)

text2 = 'XYZ'.join(text1.split())
print('text2:',text2)
```

The `split()` function "splits" a text string into a set of words, and also removes the extraneous white spaces. Next, the `join()` function "joins" together the words in the string `text1`, using a single white space as the delimiter. The last code portion of the preceding code block uses the string `XYZ` as the delimiter instead of a single white space.

The output of the preceding code block is here:

```
text1:    there are    extra   spaces
text2: there are extra spaces
text2: thereXYZareXYZextraXYZspaces
```

PYTHON `while` LOOPS

You can define a `while` loop to iterate through a set of numbers, as shown in the following examples:

```
>>> x = 0
>>> while x < 5:
...     print(x)
...     x = x + 1
...
0
1
2
3
4
5
```

`Python` uses indentation instead of curly braces that are used in other languages such as JavaScript and Java. Although `Python` lists are not discussed until Chapter 3, you can probably understand the following simple code block that contains a variant of the preceding loop that you can use when working with lists:

```
lst  = [1,2,3,4]

while lst:
  print('list:',lst)
  print('item:',lst.pop())
```

The preceding `while` loop terminates when the `lst` variable is empty, and there is no need to explicitly test for an empty list. The output from the preceding code is here:

```
list: [1, 2, 3, 4]
item: 4
list: [1, 2, 3]
item: 3
list: [1, 2]
item: 2
list: [1]
item: 1
```

This concludes the examples that use the `split()` function in order to process words and characters in a text string. The next part of this chapter shows you examples of using conditional logic in Python code.

CONDITIONAL LOGIC IN PYTHON

If you have written code in other programming languages, you have undoubtedly seen `if/then/else` (or `if-elseif-else`) conditional statements. Although the syntax varies between languages, the logic is essentially the same. The following example shows you how to use `if/elif` statements in `Python`:

```
>>> x = 25
>>> if x < 0:
...     print('negative')
... elif x < 25:
...     print('under 25')
... elif x == 25:
...     print('exactly 25')
... else:
...     print('over 25')
...
exactly 25
```

The preceding code block illustrates how to use multiple conditional statements, and the output is exactly what you expected.

THE break/continue/pass STATEMENTS

The break statement in Python enables you to perform an "early exit" from a loop, whereas the continue statement essentially returns to the top of the loop and continues with the next value of the loop variable. The pass statement is essentially a "do nothing" statement.

Listing 2.9 displays the contents of BreakContinuePass.py that illustrates the use of these three statements.

LISTING 2.9: BreakContinuePass.py

```
print('first loop')
for x in range(1,4):
  if(x == 2):
    break
  print(x)

print('second loop')
for x in range(1,4):
  if(x == 2):
    continue
  print(x)

print('third loop')
for x in range(1,4):
  if(x == 2):
    pass
  print(x)
```

The output of Listing 2.9 is here:

```
first loop
1
second loop
1
3
third loop
1
2
3
```

COMPARISON AND BOOLEAN OPERATORS

Python supports a variety of Boolean operators, such as in, not in, is, is not, and, or, and not. The next several sections discuss these operators and provide some examples of how to use them.

The in/not in/is/is not Comparison Operators

The in and not in operators are used with sequences to check whether a value occurs or does not occur in a sequence. The operators is and is not determine whether or not two objects are the same object, which is important only matters for mutable objects such as lists. All comparison operators have the same priority, which is lower than that of all numerical operators. Comparisons can also be chained. For example, a < b == c tests whether a is less than b and moreover b equals c.

The and, or, and not Boolean Operators

The Boolean operators and, or, and not have lower priority than comparison operators. The Boolean and and or are binary operators whereas the Boolean or operator is a unary operator. Here are some examples:

- A and B can only be true if both A and B are true
- A or B is true if either A or B is true
- not (A) is true if and only if A is false

You can also assign the result of a comparison or other Boolean expression to a variable, as shown here:

```
>>> string1, string2, string3 = '', 'b', 'cd'
>>> str4 = string1 or string2 or string3
>>> str4
'b'
```

The preceding code block initializes the variables string1, string2, and string3, where string1 is an empty string. Next, str4 is initialized via the or operator, and since the first nonnull value is string2, the value of str4 is equal to string2.

LOCAL AND GLOBAL VARIABLES

Python variables can be local or global. A Python variable is local to a function if the following are true:

- a parameter of the function
- on the left-side of a statement in the function
- bound to a control structure (such as for, with, and except)

A variable that is referenced in a function but is not local (according to the previous list) is a nonlocal variable. You can specify a variable as nonlocal with this snippet:

```
nonlocal z
```

A variable can be explicitly declared as global with this statement:

```
global z
```

The following code block illustrates the behavior of a global versus a local variable:

```
global z
z = 3

def changeVar(z):
  z = 4
  print('z in function:',z)

print('first global z:',z)

if __name__ == '__main__':
  changeVar(z)
  print('second global z:',z)
```

The output from the preceding code block is here:

```
first global z: 3
z in function: 4
second global z: 3
```

Uninitialized Variables and the Value None

Python distinguishes between an uninitialized variable and the value None. The former is a variable that has not been assigned a value, whereas the value None is a value that indicates "no value" Collections and methods often return the value None, and you can test for the value None in conditional logic.

SCOPE OF VARIABLES

The accessibility or scope of a variable depends on where that variable has been defined. Python provides two scopes: global and local, with the added "twist" that global is actually module-level scope (i.e., the current file), and therefore you can have a variable with the same name in different files and they will be treated differently.

Local variables are straightforward: they are defined inside a function, and they can only be accessed inside the function where they are defined. Any variables that are not local variables have global scope, which means that those variables are "global" *only* with respect to the file where it has been defined, and they can be accessed anywhere in a file.

There are two scenarios to consider regarding variables. First, suppose two files (aka modules) file1.py and file2.py have a variable called x, and file1.py also imports file2.py. The question now is how to disambiguate between the x in the two different modules. As an example, suppose that file2.py contains the following two lines of code:

```
x = 3
print('unscoped x in file2:',x)
```

Suppose that file1.py contains the following code:

```
import file2 as file2

x = 5
print('unscoped x in file1:',x)
print('scoped x from file2:',file2.x)
```

Launch file1.y from the command line, and you will see the following output:

```
unscoped x in file2: 3
unscoped x in file1: 5
scoped x from file2: 3
```

The second scenario involves a program that contains a local variable and a global variable with the same name. According to the earlier rule, the local variable is used in the function where it is defined, and the global variable is used outside of that function.

The following code block illustrates the use of a global and local variable with the same name:

```
#!/usr/bin/python
# a global variable:
total = 0;

def sum(x1, x2):
    # this total is local:
    total = x1+x2;

    print("Local total : ", total)
    return total

# invoke the sum function
sum(2,3);
print("Global total : ", total)
```

When the above code is executed, it produces following result:

```
Local total :    5
Global total :   0
```

What about unscoped variables, such as specifying the variable x without a module prefix? The answer consists of the following sequence of steps that Python will perform:

1. Check the local scope for the name.
2. Ascend the enclosing scopes and check for the name.
3. Perform Step 2 until the global scope is found (i.e., module level)
4. If x still hasn't been found, Python checks __builtins__.

As an illustration, type python at the command line and then enter the statements that are preceded with three angle brackets ("> > >"):

```
Python 3.9.1 (v3.9.1:1e5d33e9b9, Dec  7 2020, 12:44:01)
[Clang 12.0.0 (clang-1200.0.32.27)] on darwin
Type "help", "copyright", "credits" or "license" for more
information.
>>> x = 1
>>> g = globals()
>>> g
{'__name__': '__main__', '__doc__': None, '__package__':
None, '__loader__': <class '_frozen_importlib.
BuiltinImporter'>, '__spec__': None, '__annotations__': {},
'__builtins__': <module 'builtins' (built-in)>, 'x': 1,
'g': {...}}
>>> g.pop('x')
1
>>> x
Traceback (most recent call last):
  File "<stdin>", line 1, in <module>
NameError: name 'x' is not defined
```

NOTE · *You can access the* dicts *that Python uses to track local and global scope by invoking* locals() *and* globals() *respectively.*

PASS BY REFERENCE VERSUS VALUE

All parameters (arguments) in the Python language are passed by reference. Thus, if you change what a parameter refers to within a function, the change is reflected in the calling function. For example:

```
def changeme(mylist):
    #This changes a passed list into this function
    mylist.append([1,2,3,4])
    print("Values inside the function: ", mylist)
    return

# Now you can call changeme function
mylist = [10,20,30]
changeme(mylist)
print("Values outside the function: ", mylist)
```

Here we are maintaining reference of the passed object and appending values in the same object, and the result is shown here:

```
Values inside the function:  [10, 20, 30, [1, 2, 3, 4]]
Values outside the function:  [10, 20, 30, [1, 2, 3, 4]]
```

The fact that values are passed by reference gives rise to the notion of mutability versus immutability that is discussed in Chapter 3.

ARGUMENTS AND PARAMETERS

Python differentiates between arguments to functions and parameter declarations in functions: a positional (mandatory) and keyword (optional/default value). This concept is important because Python has operators for packing and unpacking these kinds of arguments.

Python unpacks positional arguments from an iterable, as shown here:

```
>>> def foo(x, y):
...     return x - y
...
>>> data = 4,5
>>> foo(data) # only passed one arg
Traceback (most recent call last):
  File "<stdin>", line 1, in <module>
TypeError: foo() takes exactly 2 arguments (1 given)
>>> foo(*data) # passed however many args are in tuple
-1
```

USING A while LOOP TO FIND THE DIVISORS OF A NUMBER

Listing 2.10 contains a while loop, conditional logic, and the % (modulus) operator in order to find the factors of any integer greater than 1.

LISTING 2.10: Divisors.py

```
def divisors(num):
  div = 2

  while(num > 1):
    if(num % div == 0):
      print("divisor: ", div)
      num = num / div
    else:
      div = div + 1
  print("** finished **")

divisors(12)
```

Listing 2.10 defines a function divisors() that takes an integer value num and then initializes the variable div with the value 2. The while loop divides num by div and if the remainder is 0, it prints the value of div and then it divides num by div; if the value is not 0, then div is incremented by 1. This while loop continues as long as the value of num is greater than 1.

The output from Listing 2.10 passing in the value 12 to the function divisors() is here:

```
divisor:  2
divisor:  2
divisor:  3
** finished **
```

Listing 2.11 displays the contents of Divisors2.py that contains a while loop, conditional logic, and the % (modulus) operator in order to find the factors of any integer greater than 1.

LISTING 2.11: Divisors2.py

```python
def divisors(num):
  primes = ""
  div = 2

  while(num > 1):
    if(num % div == 0):
      divList = divList + str(div) + ' '
      num = num / div
    else:
      div = div + 1
  return divList

result = divisors(12)
print('The divisors of',12,'are:',result)
```

Listing 2.11 is very similar to Listing 2.10: the main difference is that Listing 2.10 constructs the variable `divList` (which is a concatenated list of the divisors of a number) in the `while` loop, and then returns the value of `divList` when the `while` loop has completed. The output from Listing 2.11 is here:

```
The divisors of 12 are: 2 2 3
```

Using a `while` loop to Find Prime Numbers

Listing 2.12 displays the contents of `Divisors3.py` that contains a `while` loop, conditional logic, and the % (modulus) operator in order to count the number of prime factors of any integer greater than 1. If there is only one divisor for a number, then that number is a prime number.

LISTING 2.12: Divisors3.py

```python
def divisors(num):
  count = 1
  div = 2
  while(div < num):
    if(num % div == 0):
      count = count + 1
    div = div + 1
  return count

result = divisors(12)

if(result == 1):
  print('12 is prime')
else:
  print('12 is not prime')
```

USER-DEFINED FUNCTIONS IN PYTHON

Python provides built-in functions and also enables you to define your own functions. You can define functions to provide the required functionality. Here are simple rules to define a function in Python:

- Function blocks begin with the keyword def followed by the function name and parentheses.
- Any input arguments should be placed within these parentheses.
- The first statement of a function can be an optional statement—the documentation string of the function or docstring.
- The code block within every function starts with a colon (:) and is indented.
- The statement return [expression] exits a function, optionally passing back an expression to the caller. A return statement with no arguments is the same as return "None."
- If a function does not specify a return statement, the function automatically returns "None," which is a special type of value in Python.

A very simple custom Python function is here:

```
>>> def func():
...     print 3
...
>>> func()
3
```

The preceding function is trivial, but it does illustrate the syntax for defining custom functions in Python. The following example is slightly more useful:

```
>>> def func(x):
...     for i in range(0,x):
...         print(i)
...
>>> func(5)
0
1
2
3
4
```

SPECIFYING DEFAULT VALUES IN A FUNCTION

Listing 2.13 displays the contents of DefaultValues.py that illustrates how to specify default values in a function.

LISTING 2.13: DefaultValues.py

```
def numberFunc(a, b=10):
  print (a,b)

def stringFunc(a, b='xyz'):
  print (a,b)

def collectionFunc(a, b=None):
  if(b is None):
      print('No value assigned to b')

numberFunc(3)
stringFunc('one')
collectionFunc([1,2,3])
```

Listing 2.13 defines three functions, followed by an invocation of each of those functions. The functions `numberFunc()` and `stringFunc()` print a list containing the values of their two parameters, and `collectionFunc()` displays a message if the second parameter is `None`. The output from Listing 2.13 is here:

```
(3, 10)
('one', 'xyz')
No value assigned to b
```

Returning Multiple Values From a Function

This task is accomplished by the code in Listing 2.14, which displays the contents of `MultipleValues.py`.

LISTING 2.14: MultipleValues.py

```
def MultipleValues():
    return 'a', 'b', 'c'

x, y, z = MultipleValues()

print('x:',x)
print('y:',y)
print('z:',z)
```

The output from Listing 2.14 is here:

```
x: a
y: b
z: c
```

FUNCTIONS WITH A VARIABLE NUMBER OF ARGUMENTS

`Python` enables you to define functions with a variable number of arguments. This functionality is useful in many situations, such as computing the sum, average, or product of a set of numbers. For example, the following code block computes the sum of two numbers:

```
def sum(a, b):
    return a + b
```

```
values = (1, 2)
s1 = sum(*values)
print('s1 = ', s1)
```

The output of the preceding code block is here:

```
s1 =  3
```

However, the sum function in the preceding code block can only be used for two numeric values.

Listing 2.15 displays the contents of VariableSum1.py that illustrates how to compute the sum of a variable number of numbers.

LISTING 2.15: VariableSum1.py

```
def sum(*values):
  sum = 0
  for x in values:
    sum = sum + x
  return sum

values1 = (1, 2)
s1 = sum(*values1)
print('s1 = ',s1)

values2 = (1, 2, 3, 4)
s2 = sum(*values2)
print('s2 = ',s2)
```

Listing 2.15 defines the function sum whose parameter values can be an arbitrary list of numbers. The next portion of this function initializes sum to 0, and then a for loop iterates through values and adds each of its elements to the variable sum. The last line in the function sum() returns the value of the variable sum. The output from Listing 2.15 is here:

```
s1 =  3
s2 =  10
```

LAMBDA EXPRESSIONS

Listing 2.16 displays the contents of Lambda1.py that illustrates how to create a simple lambda function in Python.

LISTING 2.16 Lambda1.py

```
add = lambda x, y: x + y

x1 = add(5,7)
x2 = add('Hello', 'Python')

print(x1)
print(x2)
```

Listing 2.16 defines the lambda expression add that accepts two input parameters and then returns their sum (for numbers) or their concatenation (for strings).

The output from Listing 2.16 is here:

```
12
HelloPython
```

RECURSION

Recursion is a powerful technique that can provide an elegant solution to various problems. The following subsections contain examples of using recursion to calculate some well-known numbers.

Calculating Factorial Values

The factorial value of a positive integer n is the product of all the integers between 1 and n. The symbol for factorial is the exclamation point ("!") and some sample factorial values are here:

```
1! = 1
2! = 2
3! = 6
4! = 20
5! = 120
```

The formula for the factorial value of a number is succinctly defined as follows:

```
Factorial(n) = n*Factorial(n-1) for n > 1 and Factorial(1) = 1
```

Listing 2.17 displays the contents of Factorial.py that illustrates how to use recursion in order to calculate the factorial value of a positive integer.

LISTING 2.17: Factorial.py

```
def factorial(num):
    if (num > 1):
        return num * factorial(num-1)
    else:
        return 1

result = factorial(5)
print('The factorial of 5 =', result)
```

Listing 2.17 contains the function factorial that implements the recursive definition of the factorial value of a number. The output from Listing 2.17 is here:

```
The factorial of 5 = 120
```

In addition to a recursive solution, there is also an iterative solution for calculating the factorial value of a number. Listing 2.18 displays the contents of Factorial2.py that illustrates how to use the range() function in order to calculate the factorial value of a positive integer.

LISTING 2.18: Factorial2.py

```
def factorial2(num):
  prod = 1
  for x in range(1,num+1):
    prod = prod * x
  return prod

result = factorial2(5)
print 'The factorial of 5 =', result
```

Listing 2.18 defines the function factorial2() with a parameter num, followed by the variable prod which has an initial value of 1. The next part of factorial2() is a for loop whose loop variable x ranges between 1 and num+1, and each iteration through that loop multiples the value of prod with the value of x, thereby computing the factorial value of num. The output from Listing 2.18 is here:

```
The factorial of 5 = 120
```

Calculating Fibonacci Numbers

The set of Fibonacci numbers represent some interesting patterns (such as the pattern of a sunflower) in nature, and its recursive definition is here:

```
Fib(0)  = 0
Fib(1)  = 1
Fib(n)  = Fib(n-1) + Fib(n-2) for n >= 2
```

Listing 2.19 displays the contents of fib.py that illustrates how to calculate Fibonacci numbers.

LISTING 2.19: fib.py

```
def fib(num):
  if (num == 0):
    return 1
  elif (num == 1):
    return 1
  else:
    return fib(num-1) + fib(num-2)

result = fib(10)
print('Fibonacci value of 5 =', result)
```

Listing 2.19 defines the fib() function with the parameter num. If num equals 0 or 1 then fib() returns num; otherwise, fib() returns the result of adding fib(num-1) and fib(num-2). The output from Listing 2.19 is here:

```
Fibonacci value of 10 = 89
```

Calculating the GCD of Two Numbers

The GCD (greatest common divisor) of two positive integers is the largest integer that divides both integers with a remainder of 0. Some values are shown here:

```
gcd(6,2)   = 2
gcd(10,4)  = 2
gcd(24,16) = 8
```

Listing 2.20 uses recursion and Euclid's algorithm in order to find the GCD of two positive integers.

LISTING: 2.20 gcd.py

```
def gcd(num1, num2):
   if(num1 % num2 == 0):
      return num2
   elif (num1 < num2):
      print("switching ", num1, " and ", num2)
      return gcd(num2, num1)
   else:
      print("reducing", num1, " and ", num2)
      return gcd(num1-num2, num2)

result = gcd(24, 10)
print("GCD of", 24, "and", 10, "=", result)
```

Listing 2.20 defines the function gcd() with the parameters num1 and num2. If num1 is divisible by num2, the function returns num2. If num1 is less than num2, then gcd is invoked by switching the order of num1 and num2. In all other cases, gcd() returns the result of computing gcd() with the values num1-num2 and num2. The output from Listing 2.20 is here:

```
reducing 24   and   10
reducing 14   and   10
switching  4   and   10
reducing 10   and   4
reducing 6   and   4
switching  2   and   4
GCD of 24 and 10 = 2
```

Calculating the LCM of Two Numbers

The LCM (lowest common multiple) of two positive integers is the smallest integer that is a multiple of those two integers. Some values are shown here:

```
lcm(6,2)   = 2
lcm(10,4)  = 20
lcm(24,16) = 48
```

In general, if x and y are two positive integers, you can calculate their LCM as follows:

```
lcm(x,y) = x/gcd(x,y)*y/gcd(x,y)
```

Listing 2.21 uses the gcd() function that is defined in the previous section in order to calculate the LCM of two positive integers.

LISTING 2.21: lcm.py

```
def gcd(num1, num2):
  if(num1 % num2 == 0):
    return num2
  elif (num1 < num2):
   #print("switching ", num1, " and ", num2)
    return gcd(num2, num1)
  else:
   #print("reducing", num1, " and ", num2)
    return gcd(num1-num2, num2)

def lcm(num1, num2):
  gcd1 = gcd(num1, num2)
  lcm1 = num1*num2/gcd1
  return lcm1

result = lcm(24, 10)
print("The LCM of", 24, "and", 10, "=", result)
```

Listing 2.21 defines the function gcd() that was discussed in the previous section, followed by the function lcm that takes the parameters num1 and num2. The first line in lcm() computes gcd1, which is the gcd() of num1 and num2. The second line in lcm() computes lcm1, which is num1 divided by three values. The third line in lcm() returns the value of lcm1. The output of Listing 2.21 is here:

```
The LCM of 24 and 10 = 60
```

SUMMARY

This chapter showed you how to use conditional logic in Python. You also learned how to work with loops in Python, including for loops and while loops. You learned how to compute various values, such as the GCD (greatest common divisor) and LCM (lowest common multiple) of a pair of numbers, and also how to determine whether or not a positive integer is prime.

## CHAPTER 3

PYTHON DATA STRUCTURES

In Chapters 1 and 2, you learned how to work with numbers and strings, as well as control structures in Python. This chapter discusses Python collections, such as lists (or arrays), sets, tuples, and dictionaries. You will see many short code blocks that will help you rapidly learn how to work with these data structures in Python. After you have finished reading this chapter, you will be in a better position to create more complex Python modules using one or more of these data structures.

The first part of this chapter discusses Python lists and shows you code samples that illustrate various methods that are available for manipulating lists. The second part of this chapter discusses Python sets and how they differ from Python lists.

The third part of this chapter discusses Python tuples, and the final part of this chapter discusses Python dictionaries.

WORKING WITH LISTS

Python supports a list data type, along with a rich set of list-related functions. Since lists are not typed, you can create a list of different data types, as well as multidimensional lists. The next several sections show you how to manipulate list structures in Python.

Lists and Basic Operations

A Python list consists of comma-separated values enclosed in a pair of square brackets. The following examples illustrate the syntax for defining a list in Python, and also how to perform various operations on a Python list:

```
>>> list = [1, 2, 3, 4, 5]
>>> list
[1, 2, 3, 4, 5]
>>> list[2]
3
>>> list2 = list + [1, 2, 3, 4, 5]
>>> list2
[1, 2, 3, 4, 5, 1, 2, 3, 4, 5]
>>> list2.append(6)
```

```
>>> list2
[1, 2, 3, 4, 5, 1, 2, 3, 4, 5, 6]
>>> len(list)
5
>>> x = ['a', 'b', 'c']
>>> y = [1, 2, 3]
>>> z = [x, y]
>>> z[0]
['a', 'b', 'c']
>>> len(x)
3
```

You can assign multiple variables to a list, provided that the number and type of the variables match the structure. Here is an example:

```
>>> point = [7,8]
>>> x,y = point
>>> x
7
>>> y
8
```

The following example shows you how to assign values to variables from a more complex data structure:

```
>>> line = ['a', 10, 20, (2014,01,31)]
>>> x1,x2,x3,date1 = line
>>> x1
'a'
>>> x2
10
>>> x3
20
>>> date1
(2014, 1, 31)
```

If you want to access the year/month/date components of the date1 element in the preceding code block, you can do so with the following code block:

```
>>> line = ['a', 10, 20, (2014,01,31)]
>>> x1,x2,x3,(year,month,day) = line
>>> x1
'a'
>>> x2
10
>>> x3
20
>>> year
2014
>>> month
1
>>> day
31
```

If the number and/or structure of the variables do not match the data, an error message is displayed, as shown here:

```
>>> point = (1,2)
>>> x,y,z = point
Traceback (most recent call last):
```

```
   File "<stdin>", line 1, in <module>
ValueError: need more than 2 values to unpack
```

If the number of variables that you specify is less than the number of data items, you will see an error message, as shown here:

```
>>> line = ['a', 10, 20, (2014,01,31)]
>>> x1,x2 = line
Traceback (most recent call last):
   File "<stdin>", line 1, in <module>
ValueError: too many values to unpack
```

Reversing and Sorting a List

The Python `reverse()` method reverses the contents of a list, as shown here:

```
>>> a = [4, 1, 2, 3]
>>> a.reverse()
[3, 2, 1, 4]
```

The Python `sort()` method sorts a list:

```
>>> a = [4, 1, 2, 3]
>>> a.sort()
[1, 2, 3, 4]
```

You can sort a list and then reverse its contents, as shown here:

```
>>> a = [4, 1, 2, 3]
>>> a.reverse(a.sort())
[4, 3, 2, 1]
```

Another way to reverse a list is as follows:

```
>>> L = [0,10,20,40]
>>> L[::-1]
[40, 20, 10, 0]
```

Keep in mind is that `reversed(array)` is an iterable and not a list. However, you can convert the reversed array to a list with this code snippet:

```
list(reversed(array)) or L[::-1]
```

Listing 3.1 contains a `while` loop whose logic is the opposite of the listing in the previous section: if num is divisible by multiple numbers (each of which is strictly less than num), then num is not prime.

LISTING 3.1: Uppercase1.py

```
list1 = ['a', 'list', 'of', 'words']
list2 = [s.upper() for s in list1]
list3 = [s for s in list1 if len(s) <=2 ]
list4 = [s for s in list1 if 'w' in s ]
```

```
print ('list1:',list1)
print ('list2:',list2)
print ('list3:',list3)
print ('list4:',list4)
```

The output from launching the code in Listing 3.1 is here:

```
list1: ['a', 'list', 'of', 'words']
list2: ['A', 'LIST', 'OF', 'WORDS']
list3: ['a', 'of']
list4: ['words']
```

Lists and Arithmetic Operations

The minimum value of a list of numbers is the first number of in the sorted list of numbers. If you reverse the sorted list, the first number is the maximum value. There are several ways to reverse a list, starting with the technique shown in the following code:

```
x = [3,1,2,4]
maxList = x.sort()
minList = x.sort(x.reverse())

min1 = min(x)
max1 = max(x)
print(min1)
print(max1)
```

The output of the preceding code block is here:

```
1
4
```

A second (and better) way to sort a list is shown here:

```
minList = x.sort(reverse=True)
```

A third way to sort a list involves the built-in functional version of the sort() method, as shown here:

```
sorted(x, reverse=True)
```

The preceding code snippet is useful when you do not want to modify the original order of the list or you want to compose multiple list operations on a single line.

Lists and Filter-Related Operations

Python enables you to filter a list (also called list comprehension), as shown here:

```
mylist = [1, -2, 3, -5, 6, -7, 8]
pos = [n for n in mylist if n > 0]
neg = [n for n in mylist if n < 0]
```

```
print(pos)
print(neg)
```

You can also specify if/else logic in a filter, as shown here:

```
mylist = [1, -2, 3, -5, 6, -7, 8]
negativeList = [n if n < 0 else 0 for n in mylist]
positiveList = [n if n > 0 else 0 for n in mylist]

print(positiveList)
print(negativeList)
```

The output of the preceding code block is here:

```
[1, 3, 6, 8]
[-2, -5, -7]
[1, 0, 3, 0, 6, 0, 8]
[0, -2, 0, -5, 0, -7, 0]
```

SORTING LISTS OF NUMBERS AND STRINGS

Listing 3.2 displays the content of the Python script Sorted1.py that determines whether two lists are sorted.

LISTING 3.2: Sorted1.py

```
list1 = [1,2,3,4,5]
list2 = [2,1,3,4,5]

sort1 = sorted(list1)
sort2 = sorted(list2)

if(list1 == sort1):
  print(list1,'is sorted')
else:
  print(list1,'is not sorted')

if(list2 == sort2):
  print(list2,'is sorted')
else:
  print(list2,'is not sorted')
```

Listing 3.2 initializes the lists list1 and list2, and the sorted lists sort1 and sort2 based on the lists list1 and list2, respectively. If list1 equals sort1, then list1 is already sorted; similarly, if list2 equals sort2, then list2 is already sorted.

The output from Listing 3.2 is here:

```
[1, 2, 3, 4, 5] is sorted
[2, 1, 3, 4, 5] is not sorted
```

Note that if you sort a list of character strings, the output is case sensitive, and that uppercase letters appear before lowercase letters. This is due to the fact that the collating sequence for ASCII places uppercase letters (decimal 65 through decimal 91) before lowercase letters (decimal 97 through decimal 127). The following example provides an illustration:

```
>>> list1 = ['a', 'A', 'b', 'B', 'Z']
>>> print(sorted(list1))
['A', 'B', 'Z', 'a', 'b']
```

You can also specify the reverse option so that the list is sorted in reverse order:

```
>>> list1 = ['a', 'A', 'b', 'B', 'Z']
>>> print(sorted(list1, reverse=True))
['b', 'a', 'Z', 'B', 'A']
```

You can even sort a list based on the length of the items in the list:

```
>>> list1 = ['a', 'AA', 'bbb', 'BBBBB', 'ZZZZZZZ']
>>> print (sorted(list1, key=len))
['a', 'AA', 'bbb', 'BBBBB', 'ZZZZZZZ']
>>> print(sorted(list1, key=len, reverse=True))
['ZZZZZZZ', 'BBBBB', 'bbb', 'AA', 'a']
```

You can specify `str.lower` if you want treat uppercase letters as though they are lowercase letters during the sorting operation, as shown here:

```
>>> print(sorted(list1, key=str.lower))
['a', 'AA', 'bbb', 'BBBBB', 'ZZZZZZZ']
```

EXPRESSIONS IN LISTS

The following construct is similar to a `for` loop but without the colon ":" character that appears at the end of a loop construct. Consider the following example:

```
nums = [1, 2, 3, 4]
cubes = [ n*n*n for n in nums ]

print('nums: ',nums)
print('cubes:',cubes)
```

The output from the preceding code block is here:

```
nums:  [1, 2, 3, 4]
cubes: [1, 8, 27, 64]
```

CONCATENATING A LIST OF WORDS

Python provides the `join()` method for concatenating text strings, as shown here:

```
>>> parts = ['Is', 'SF', 'In', 'California?']
>>> ' '.join(parts)
'Is SF In California?'
>>> ','.join(parts)
'Is,SF,In,California?'
>>> ''.join(parts) 'IsSFInCalifornia?'
```

There are several ways to concatenate a set of strings and then print the result. The following is the most *inefficient* way to do so:

```
print("This" + "is" + "a" + "sentence")
```

Either of the following is preferred:

```
print("%s %s %s %s" % ("This", "is", "a", "sentence"))
print(" ".join(["This","is","a","sentence"]))
```

THE BUBBLE SORT IN PYTHON

The previous sections contain examples that illustrate how to sort a list of numbers using the sort() function. However, sometimes you need to implement different types of sorts in Python. Listing 3.3 displays the content of BubbleSort.py that illustrates how to implement the bubble sort in Python.

LISTING 3.3: BubbleSort.py

```
list1 = [1, 5, 3, 4]

print("Initial list:",list1)

for i in range(0,len(list1)-1):
  for j in range(i+1,len(list1)):
    if(list1[i] > list1[j]):
      temp = list1[i]
      list1[i] = list1[j]
      list1[j] = temp

print("Sorted list: ",list1)
```

The output from Listing 3.3 is here:

```
Initial list: [1, 5, 3, 4]
Sorted list:  [1, 3, 4, 5]
```

THE PYTHON RANGE() FUNCTION

In this section, you will learn about the Python range() function, which you can use to iterate through a list, as shown here:

```
>>> for i in range(0,5):
...     print(i)
```

```
. . .
0
1
2
3
4
```

You can use a `for` loop to iterate through a list of strings, as shown here:

```
>>> x
['a', 'b', 'c']
>>> for w in x:
...     print(w)
...
a
b
c
```

You can use a `for` loop to iterate through a list of strings and provide additional details, as shown here:

```
>>> x
['a', 'b', 'c']
>>> for w in x:
...     print(len(w), w)
...
1 a
1 b
1 c
```

The preceding output displays the length of each word in the list x, followed by the word itself.

Counting Digits and Uppercase and Lowercase Letters

Listing 3.4 displays the content of the Python file `CountCharTypes.py` that counts the occurrences of digits and letters in a string.

LISTING 3.4: Counter1.py

```
str1 = "abc4234AFde"
digitCount = 0
alphaCount = 0
upperCount = 0
lowerCount = 0

for i in range(0,len(str1)):
  char = str1[i]
  if(char.isdigit()):
   #print("this is a digit:",char)
    digitCount += 1
  elif(char.isalpha()):
   #print("this is alphabetic:",char)
    alphaCount  += 1
```

```
   if(char.upper() == char):
      upperCount += 1
   else:
      lowerCount += 1

print('Original String:   ',str1)
print('Number of digits:  ',digitCount)
print('Total alphanumeric:',alphaCount)
print('Upper Case Count:  ',upperCount)
print('Lower Case Count:  ',lowerCount)
```

Listing 3.4 initializes counter-related variables, followed by a loop (with loop variable i) that iterates from 0 to the length of the string str1. The string variable char is initialized with the letter at index i of the string str1. The next portion of the loop uses conditional logic to determine whether char is a digit or an alphabetic character; in the latter case, the code checks whether the character is uppercase or lowercase. In all cases, the values of the appropriate counter-related variables are incremented.

The output of Listing 3.4 is here:

```
Original String:     abc4234AFde
Number of digits:    4
Total alphanumeric:  7
Upper Case Count:    2
Lower Case Count:    5
```

ARRAYS AND THE APPEND() FUNCTION

Python does have an array type (import array), which is very good for numeric calculations, as well as a slight saving in memory use. You can also define heterogeneous arrays:

```
a = [10, 'hello', [5, '77']]
```

You can append a new element to an element inside a list:

```
>>> a = [10, 'hello', [5, '77']]
>>> a[2].append('abc')
>>> a
[10, 'hello', [5, '77', 'abc']]
```

You can assign simple variables to the elements of a list, as shown here:

```
myList = [ 'a', 'b', 91.1, (2014, 01, 31) ]
x1, x2, x3, x4 = myList
print('x1:',x1)
print('x2:',x2)
print('x3:',x3)
print('x4:',x4)
```

The output of the preceding code block is here:

```
x1: a
x2: b
x3: 91.1
x4: (2014, 1, 31)
```

The Python `split()` function is more convenient (especially when the number of elements is unknown or variable) than the preceding sample, and you will see examples of the `split()` function in the next section.

WORKING WITH LISTS AND THE SPLIT() FUNCTION

You can use the Python `split()` function to split the words in a text string and populate a list with those words. An example is here:

```
>>> x = "this is a string"
>>> list = x.split()
>>> list
['this', 'is', 'a', 'string']
```

A simple way to print the list of words in a text string is shown here:

```
>>> x = "this is a string"
>>> for w in x.split():
...     print(w)
...
this
is
a
string
```

You can search for a word in a string as follows:

```
>>> x = "this is a string"
>>> for w in x.split():
...     if(w == 'this'):
...         print("x contains this")
...
x contains this
...
```

COUNTING WORDS IN A LIST

Python provides the `Counter` class, which enables you to count the words in a list. Listing 3.5 shows the content of `CountWord2.py` that displays the top three words with the greatest frequency.

LISTING 3.5: CountWord2.py

```
from collections import Counter
```

```
mywords = ['a', 'b', 'a', 'b', 'c', 'a', 'd', 'e', 'f', 'b']

word_counts = Counter(mywords)
topThree = word_counts.most_common(3)
print(topThree)
```

Listing 3.5 initializes the variable `mywords` with a set of characters and then initializes the variable `word_counts` by passing `mywords` as an argument to `Counter`. The variable `topThree` is an array containing the three most common characters (and their frequency) that appear in `mywords`. The output from Listing 3.5 is here:

```
[('a', 3), ('b', 3), ('c', 1)]
```

ITERATING THROUGH PAIRS OF LISTS

Python supports operations on pairs of lists, which means that you can perform vector-like operations. The following snippet multiplies every list element by 3:

```
>>> list1 = [1, 2, 3]
>>> [3*x for x in list1]
[3, 6, 9]
```

Create a new list with pairs of elements consisting of the original element and the original element multiplied by 3 with the following code:

```
>>> list1 = [1, 2, 3]
>>> [[x, 3*x] for x in list1]
[[1, 3], [2, 6], [3, 9]]
```

Compute the product of every pair of numbers from two lists with the following code:

```
>>> list1 = [1, 2, 3]
>>> list2 = [5, 6, 7]
>>> [a*b for a in list1 for b in list2]
[5, 6, 7, 10, 12, 14, 15, 18, 21]
```

Calculate the sum of every pair of numbers from two lists with the following code:

```
>>> list1 = [1, 2, 3]
>>> list2 = [5, 6, 7]
>>> [a+b for a in list1 for b in list2]
[6, 7, 8, 7, 8, 9, 8, 9, 10]
```

Calculate the pair-wise product of two lists with the following code:

```
>>> [list1[i]*list2[i] for i in range(len(list1))]

[5, 12, 21]
```

OTHER LIST-RELATED FUNCTIONS

Python provides additional functions that you can use with lists, such as `append()`, `insert()`, `delete()`, `pop()`, and `extend()`. Python also supports the functions `index()`, `count()`, `sort()`, and `reverse()`. Examples of these functions are illustrated in the following code block.

Define a Python list (notice that duplicates are allowed):

```
>>> a = [1, 2, 3, 2, 4, 2, 5]
```

Display the number of occurrences of 1 and 2:

```
>>> print(a.count(1), a.count(2))
1 3
```

Insert -8 in position 3:

```
>>> a.insert(3,-8)
>>> a
[1, 2, 3, -8, 2, 4, 2, 5]
```

Remove occurrences of 3:

```
>>> a.remove(3)
>>> a
[1, 2, -8, 2, 4, 2, 5]
```

Remove occurrences of 1:

```
>>> a.remove(1)
>>> a
[2, -8, 2, 4, 2, 5]
```

Append 19 to the list:

```
>>> a.append(19)
>>> a
[2, -8, 2, 4, 2, 5, 19]
```

Print the index of 19 in the list:

```
>>> a.index(19)
6
```

Reverse the list:

```
>>> a.reverse()
>>> a
[19, 5, 2, 4, 2, -8, 2]
```

Sort the list:

```
>>> a.sort()
```

```
>>> a
[-8, 2, 2, 2, 4, 5, 19]
```

Extend list a with list b:

```
>>> b = [100,200,300]
>>> a.extend(b)
>>> a
[-8, 2, 2, 2, 4, 5, 19, 100, 200, 300]
```

Remove the first occurrence of 2:

```
>>> a.pop(2)
2
>>> a
[-8, 2, 2, 4, 5, 19, 100, 200, 300]
```

Remove the last item of the list:

```
>>> a.pop()
300
>>> a
[-8, 2, 2, 4, 5, 19, 100, 200]
```

Now that you understand how to use list-related operations, the next section shows you how to use a Python list as a stack.

USING A LIST AS A STACK AND A QUEUE

A stack is a LIFO ("Last In, First Out") data structure with push() and pop() functions for adding and removing elements, respectively. The most recently added element in a stack is in the top position, and therefore the first element that can be removed from the stack.

The following code block illustrates how to create a stack and also remove and append items from a stack in Python. Create a Python list (which we will use as a stack):

```
>>> s = [1,2,3,4]
```

Append 5 to the stack:

```
>>> s.append(5)
>>> s
[1, 2, 3, 4, 5]
```

Remove the last element from the stack:

```
>>> s.pop()
5
>>> s
[1, 2, 3, 4]
```

A queue is a FIFO ("First In, First Out") data structure with `insert()` and `pop()` functions for inserting and removing elements, respectively. The most recently added element in a queue is in the top position, and therefore the last element that can be removed from the queue.

The following code block illustrates how to create a queue and also insert and append items to a queue in Python.

Create a Python list (which we will use as a queue):

```
>>> q = [1,2,3,4]
```

Insert 5 at the beginning of the queue:

```
>>> q.insert(0,5)
>>> q
[5, 1, 2, 3, 4]
```

Remove the last element from the queue:

```
>>> q.pop(0)
1
>>> q
[5, 2, 3, 4]
```

The preceding code uses `q.insert(0, 5)` to insert in the beginning and `q.pop()` to remove from the end. However, keep in mind that the `insert()` operation is slow in Python: inserting at 0 requires copying all the elements in the underlying array down one space. Therefore, use `collections.deque` with `coll.appendleft()` and `coll.pop()`, where `coll` is an instance of the `Collection` class.

The next section shows you how to work with vectors in Python.

WORKING WITH VECTORS

A vector is a one-dimensional array of values, and you can perform vector-based operations, such as addition, subtraction, and inner product. Listing 3.6 displays the content of `MyVectors.py` that illustrates how to perform vector-based operations.

LISTING 3.6: MyVectors.py

```
v1 = [1,2,3]
v2 = [1,2,3]
v3 = [5,5,5]

s1 = [0,0,0]
d1 = [0,0,0]
p1 = 0

print("Initial Vectors"
print('v1:',v1)
```

```
print('v2:',v2)
print('v3:',v3)

for i in range(len(v1)):
    d1[i] = v3[i] - v2[i]
    s1[i] = v3[i] + v2[i]
    p1    = v3[i] * v2[i] + p1

print("After operations")
print('d1:',d1)
print('s1:',s1)
print('p1:',p1)
```

Listing 3.6 starts with the definition of three lists in Python, each of which represents a vector. The lists d1 and s1 represent the difference of v2 and the sum v2, respectively. The number p1 represents the "inner product" (also called the "dot product") of v3 and v2. The output from Listing 3.6 is here:

```
Initial Vectors
v1: [1, 2, 3]
v2: [1, 2, 3]
v3: [5, 5, 5]
After operations
d1: [4, 3, 2]
s1: [6, 7, 8]
p1: 30
```

WORKING WITH MATRICES

A two-dimensional matrix is a two-dimensional array of values, and you can easily create such a matrix. For example, the following code block illustrates how to access different elements in a 2D matrix:

```
mm = [["a","b","c"],["d","e","f"],["g","h","i"]];
print 'mm:     ',mm
print 'mm[0]:  ',mm[0]
print 'mm[0][1]:',mm[0][1]
```

The output from the preceding code block is here:

```
mm:        [['a', 'b', 'c'], ['d', 'e', 'f'], ['g', 'h', 'i']]
mm[0]:     ['a', 'b', 'c']
mm[0][1]: b
```

Listing 3.7 displays the content of My2DMatrix.py that illustrates how to create and populate 2 two-dimensional matrices.

LISTING 3.7: My2DMatrix.py

```
rows = 3
cols = 3
```

```
my2DMatrix = [[0 for i in range(rows)] for j in range(rows)]
print('Before:',my2DMatrix)

for row in range(rows):
  for col in range(cols):
    my2DMatrix[row][col] = row*row+col*col
print('After: ',my2DMatrix)
```

Listing 3.7 initializes the variables rows and cols, and then uses them to create the rows x cols matrix my2DMatrix, whose values are initially 0. The next part of Listing 3.7 contains a nested loop that initializes the element of my2DMatrix, whose position is (row, col) with the value row*row+col*col. The last line of code in Listing 3.7 prints the contents of my2DArray. The output from Listing 3.7 is here:

```
Before:  [[0, 0, 0], [0, 0, 0], [0, 0, 0]]
After:   [[0, 1, 4], [1, 2, 5], [4, 5, 8]]
```

THE NUMPY LIBRARY FOR MATRICES

The NumPy library (which you can install via pip) has a matrix object for manipulating matrices in Python. The following examples illustrate some of the features of NumPy.

Initialize a matrix m, and then display its contents:

```
>>> import numpy as np
>>> m = np.matrix([[1,-2,3],[0,4,5],[7,8,-9]])
>>> m
matrix([[ 1,  -2,  3],
        [ 0,   4,  5],
        [ 7,   8, -9]])
```

The next snippet returns the transpose of matrix m:

```
>>> m.T
matrix([[ 1,  0,  7],
        [-2,  4,  8],
        [ 3,  5, -9]])
```

The next snippet returns the inverse of matrix m (if it exists):

```
>>> m.I
matrix([[ 0.33043478, -0.02608696,  0.09565217],
        [-0.15217391,  0.13043478,  0.02173913],
        [ 0.12173913,  0.09565217, -0.0173913 ]])
```

The next snippet defines a vector y and then computes the product m*v:

```
>>> v = np.matrix([[2],[3],[4]])
>>> v
matrix([[2],[3],[4]])
```

```
>>> m * v
matrix([[ 8],[32],[ 2]])
```

The next snippet imports the `numpy.linalg` subpackage and then computes the determinant of the matrix m:

```
>>> import numpy.linalg
>>> numpy.linalg.det(m)
-229.99999999999983
```

The next snippet finds the eigenvalues of the matrix m:

```
>>> numpy.linalg.eigvals(m)
array([-13.11474312, 2.75956154, 6.35518158])
```

The next snippet finds solutions to the equation `m*x = v`:

```
>>> x = numpy.linalg.solve(m, v)
>>> x
matrix([[ 0.96521739],
        [ 0.17391304],
        [ 0.46086957]])
```

In addition to the preceding samples, the NumPy package provides additional functionality, which you can find by performing an Internet search for articles and tutorials.

QUEUES

A queue is a FIFO ("First In, First Out") data structure. Thus, the oldest item in a queue is removed when a new item is added to a queue that is already full.

Earlier in the chapter, you learned how to use a Python list to emulate a queue. However, there is also a queue object in Python. The following code snippets illustrate how to use a queue in Python.

```
>>> from collections import deque
>>> q = deque('',maxlen=10)
>>> for i in range(10,20):
...     q.append(i)
...
>>> print(q)
deque([10, 11, 12, 13, 14, 15, 16, 17, 18, 19], maxlen=10)
```

The next section shows you how to use tuples in Python.

TUPLES (IMMUTABLE LISTS)

Python supports a data type called a tuple that consists of comma-separated values without brackets (square brackets are for lists, round brackets are for arrays, and curly braces are for dictionaries). Various examples of Python tuples can be found online:

https://docs.python.org/3.6/tutorial/datastructures.html#tuples-and-sequences

The following code block illustrates how to create a tuple and create new tuples from an existing type in Python.

Define a Python tuple t as follows:

```
>>> t = 1,'a', 2,'hello',3
>>> t
(1, 'a', 2, 'hello', 3)
```

Display the first element of t:

```
>>> t[0]
1
```

Create a tuple v containing 10, 11, and t:

```
>>> v = 10,11,t
>>> v
(10, 11, (1, 'a', 2, 'hello', 3))
```

Try modifying an element of t (which is immutable):

```
>>> t[0] = 1000
Traceback (most recent call last):
  File "<stdin>", line 1, in <module>
TypeError: 'tuple' object does not support item assignment
```

Python "deduplication" is useful because you can remove duplicates from a set and obtain a list, as shown here:

```
>>> lst = list(set(lst))
```

NOTE *The "in" operator on a list to search is O(n) whereas the "in" operator on set is O(1).*

The next section discusses Python sets.

SETS

A Python set is an unordered collection that does not contain duplicate elements. Use curly braces or the set() function to create sets. Set objects support set-theoretic operations such as union, intersection, and difference.

NOTE *The set() function is required to create an empty set because {} creates an empty dictionary.*

The following code block illustrates how to work with a Python set. Create a list of elements:

```
>>> l = ['a', 'b', 'a', 'c']
```

Create a set from the preceding list:

```
>>> s = set(l)
>>> s
set(['a', 'c', 'b'])
```

Test if an element is in the set:

```
>>> 'a' in s
True
>>> 'd' in s
False
>>>
```

Create a set from a string:

```
>>> n = set('abacad')
>>> n
set(['a', 'c', 'b', 'd'])
>>>
```

Subtract n from s:

```
>>> s - n
set([])
```

Subtract s from n:

```
>>> n - s
set(['d'])
>>>
```

The union of s and n:

```
>>> s | n
set(['a', 'c', 'b', 'd'])
```

The intersection of s and n:

```
>>> s & n
set(['a', 'c', 'b'])
```

The exclusive-or of s and n:

```
>>> s ^ n
set(['d'])
```

The next section shows you how to work with Python dictionaries.

DICTIONARIES

Python has a key/value structure called `dict`, which is a hash table. A Python dictionary (and hash tables in general) can retrieve the value of a key in constant time, regardless of the number of entries in the dictionary (and the same is true for sets). You can think of a set as essentially just the keys (not the values) of a `dict` implementation.

The contents of a `dict` can be written as a series of `key:value` pairs, as shown here:

```
dict1 = {key1:value1, key2:value2, ... }
```

The "empty `dict`" is just an empty pair of curly braces `{}`.

Creating a Dictionary

A Python dictionary (or hash table) contains colon-separated `key:value` bindings inside a pair of curly braces, as shown here:

```
dict1 = {}
dict1 = {'x' : 1, 'y' : 2}
```

The preceding code snippet defines `dict1` as an empty dictionary, and then adds two `key:value` bindings.

Displaying the Contents of a Dictionary

You can display the contents of `dict1` with the following code:

```
>>> dict1 = {'x':1,'y':2}
>>> dict1
{'y': 2, 'x': 1}
>>> dict1['x']
1
>>> dict1['y']
2
>>> dict1['z']
Traceback (most recent call last):
  File "<stdin>", line 1, in <module>
KeyError: 'z'
```

NOTE *Key/value bindings for a `dict` and a set are not necessarily stored in the same order that you defined them.*

Python dictionaries also provide the `get` method to retrieve key values:

```
>>> dict1.get('x')
1
>>> dict1.get('y')
2
>>> dict1.get('z')
```

As you can see, the Python `get()` method returns `None` (which is displayed as an empty string) instead of an error when referencing a key that is not defined in a dictionary. You can also use `dict` comprehensions to create dictionaries from expressions, as shown here:

```
>>> {x: x**3 for x in (1, 2, 3)}
{1: 1, 2: 8, 3: 37}
```

Checking for Keys in a Dictionary

You can easily check for the presence of a key in a Python dictionary as follows:

```
>>> 'x' in dict1
True
>>> 'z' in dict1
False
```

Use square brackets for finding or setting a value in a dictionary. For example, `dict['abc']` finds the value associated with the key `'abc'`. You can use strings, numbers, and tuples work as key values, and you can use any type as the value.

If you access a value that is not in the `dict`, Python throws a `KeyError`. Consequently, use the `in` operator to check if the key is in the `dict`. Alternatively, use `dict.get(key)`, which returns the value or `None` if the key is not present. You can even use the expression `get(key, not-found-string)` to specify the value to return if a key is not found.

Deleting Keys from a Dictionary

Launch the Python interpreter and enter the following commands:

```
>>> MyDict = {'x' : 5, 'y' : 7}
>>> MyDict['z'] = 13
>>> MyDict
{'y': 7, 'x': 5, 'z': 13}
>>> del MyDict['x']
>>> MyDict
{'y': 7, 'z': 13}
>>> MyDict.keys()
['y', 'z']
>>> MyDict.values()
[13, 7]
>>> 'z' in MyDict
True
```

Iterating Through a Dictionary

The following code snippet shows you how to iterate through a dictionary:

```
MyDict = {'x' : 5, 'y' : 7, 'z' : 13}
```

```
for key, value in MyDict.items():
    print(key, value)
```

The output from the preceding code block is here:

```
y 7
x 5
z 13
```

Interpolating Data from a Dictionary

The % operator substitutes values from a Python dictionary into a string by name. Listing 3.8 contains an example of doing so.

LISTING 3.8: InterpolateDict1.py

```
hash = {}
hash['beverage'] = 'coffee'
hash['count'] = 3

# %d for int, %s for string
s = 'Today I drank %(count)d cups of %(beverage)s' % hash
print('s:', s)
```

The output from the preceding code block is here:

```
Today I drank 3 cups of coffee
```

DICTIONARY FUNCTIONS AND METHODS

Python provides various functions and methods for a dictionary, such as cmp(), len(), and str(), which compare two dictionaries, return the length of a dictionary, and display a string representation of a dictionary, respectively.

You can also manipulate the contents of a Python dictionary using the functions clear() to remove all elements, copy() to return a shallow copy, get() to retrieve the value of a key, items() to display the (key, value) pairs of a dictionary, keys() to display the keys of a dictionary, and values() to return the list of values of a dictionary.

DICTIONARY FORMATTING

The % operator substitutes values from a dict into a string by name:

```
#create a dictionary
>>> h = {}
#add a key/value pair
>>> h['item'] = 'beer'
>>> h['count'] = 4
#interpolate using %d for int, %s for string
>>> s = 'I want %(count)d bottles of %(item)s' % h
```

```
>>> s
'I want 4 bottles of beer'
```

The next section shows you how to create an ordered Python dictionary.

ORDERED DICTIONARIES

Regular Python dictionaries iterate over key/value pairs in arbitrary order. Python 2.7 introduced a new `OrderedDict` class in the `collections` module. The `OrderedDict` API provides the same interface as regular dictionaries but iterates over keys and values in a guaranteed order, depending on when a key was first inserted:

```
>>> from collections import OrderedDict
>>> d = OrderedDict([('first', 1),
...                  ('second', 2),
...                  ('third', 3)])
>>> d.items()
[('first', 1), ('second', 2), ('third', 3)]
```

If a new entry overwrites an existing entry, the original insertion position is left unchanged:

```
>>> d['second'] = 4
>>> d.items()
[('first', 1), ('second', 4), ('third', 3)]
```

Deleting an entry and reinserting it will move it to the end:

```
>>> del d['second']
>>> d['second'] = 5
>>> d.items()
[('first', 1), ('third', 3), ('second', 5)]
```

Sorting Dictionaries

Python enables you to support the entries in a dictionary. For example, you can modify the code in the preceding section to display the alphabetically sorted words and their associated word count.

Python Multi Dictionaries

You can define entries in a Python dictionary so that they reference lists or other types of Python structures. Listing 3.9 displays the content of `MultiDictionary1.py` that illustrates how to define more complex dictionaries.

LISTING 3.9: MultiDictionary1.py

```
from collections import defaultdict

d = {'a' : [1, 2, 3], 'b' : [4, 5]}
print('first:',d)
```

```
d = defaultdict(list)
d['a'].append(1)
d['a'].append(2)
d['b'].append(4)
print('second:',d)

d = defaultdict(set)
d['a'].add(1)
d['a'].add(2)
d['b'].add(4)
print('third:',d)
```

Listing 3.9 starts by defining the dictionary d and printing its contents. The next portion of Listing 3.9 specifies a list-oriented dictionary, and then modifies the values for the keys a and b. The final portion of Listing 3.9 specifies a set-oriented dictionary, and then modifies the values for the keys a and b, as well.

The output from Listing 3.9 is here:

```
first: {'a': [1, 2, 3], 'b': [4, 5]}
second: defaultdict(<type 'list'>, {'a': [1, 2], 'b': [4]})
third: defaultdict(<type 'set'>, {'a': set([1, 2]), 'b':
set([4])})
```

The next section discusses other Python sequence types that have not been discussed in previous sections of this chapter.

OTHER SEQUENCE TYPES IN PYTHON

Python supports 7 sequence types: str, unicode, list, tuple, bytearray, buffer, and xrange.

You can iterate through a sequence and retrieve the position index and corresponding value at the same time using the enumerate() function.

```
>>> for i, v in enumerate(['x', 'y', 'z']):
...     print(i, v)
...
0 x
1 y
2 z
```

Bytearray objects are created with the built-in function bytearray(). Although buffer objects are not directly supported by Python syntax, you can create them via the built-in buffer() function.

Objects of type xrange are created with the xrange() function. An xrange object is similar to a buffer in the sense that there is no specific syntax to create them. Moreover, xrange objects do not support operations such as slicing, concatenation, or repetition.

At this point, you have seen all the Python types that you will encounter in the remaining chapters of this book, so it makes sense to discuss mutable and immutable types, which is the topic of the next section.

MUTABLE AND IMMUTABLE TYPES IN PYTHON

Python represents its data as objects. Some of these objects (such as lists and dictionaries) are mutable, which means you can change their content without changing their identity. Objects such as integers, floats, strings, and tuples cannot be changed. The key point to understand is the difference between changing the value versus assigning a new value to an object; you cannot change a string, but you can assign it a different value. This detail can be verified by checking the id value of an object, as shown in Listing 3.10.

LISTING 3.10: Mutability.py

```
s = "abc"
print('id #1:', id(s))
print('first char:', s[0])

try:
  s[0] = "o"
except:
  print('Cannot perform reassignment')

s = "xyz"
print('id #2:',id(s))
s += "uvw"
print('id #3:',id(s))
```

The output of Listing 3.x is here:

```
id #1: 4297972672
first char: a
Cannot perform reassignment
id #2: 4299809336
id #3: 4299777872
```

Thus, a Python type is immutable if its value cannot be changed (even though it is possible to assign a new value to such a type), otherwise a Python type is mutable. The Python immutable objects are of type bytes, complex, float, int, str, or tuple. However, dictionaries, lists, and sets are mutable. The key in a hash table must be an immutable type.

Since strings are immutable in Python, you cannot insert a string in the "middle" of a given text string unless you construct a second string using concatenation. For example, suppose you have the string:

```
"this is a string"
```

and you want to create the following string:

```
"this is a longer string"
```

The following Python code block illustrates how to perform this task:

```
text1 = "this is a string"
text2 = text1[0:10] + "longer" + text1[9:]
print('text1:',text1)
print('text2:',text2)
```

The output of the preceding code block is here:

```
text1: this is a string
text2: this is a longer string
```

THE TYPE() FUNCTION

The `type()` primitive returns the type of any object, including Python primitives, functions, and user-defined objects. The following code sample displays the type of an integer and a string:

```
var1 = 123
var2 = 456.78
print("type var1: ",type(var1))
print("type var2: ",type(var2))
```

The output of the preceding code block is here:

```
type var1:  <type 'int'>
type var2:  <type 'float'>
```

WORKING WITH BARD

This section provides a preview of several Bard-generated Python code samples. A more comprehensive description of generative AI, Gemini, and Bard is available in Chapter 5. In addition, Chapter 6 is devoted to Bard-generated Python code samples.

The three Python code samples that you will see in subsequent sections are listed below:

• Counting Digits, Uppercase Letters, and Lowercase Letters
• Queues
• Stacks

Counting Digits and Uppercase and Lowercase Letters

The code sample that Bard generated in this section is based on the following prompt for Bard:

```
Please generate Python code that counts the number of
digits, uppercase letters, and lowercase letters in a
randomly generated string, and provide an explanation of
the Python code.
```

Listing 3.11 displays the content of `bard_count_types.py` that counts the number of occurrences of digits, uppercase letters, and lowercase letters in a randomly generated string.

The contents of Listing 3.11 (and subsequent samples in this chapter and Chapters 4 and 6) are presented "as-is:" the content and the layout are what you will see in Bard.

LISTING 3.11: bard_count_types.py

```python
import random
import string

def generate_random_string(length):
    """
    Generates a random string of specified length.

    Args:
        length: The length of the string to generate.

    Returns:
        A random string of the specified length.
    """
    letters = string.ascii_letters + string.digits
    return ''.join(random.choice(letters) for _ in
range(length))

def count_digits_uppercase_lowercase(text):
    """
    Counts the number of digits, uppercase letters, and
lowercase letters in a string.

    Args:
        text: The string to analyze.

    Returns:
        A dictionary containing the counts of digits,
uppercase letters, and lowercase letters.
    """
    digit_count = 0
    uppercase_count = 0
    lowercase_count = 0
    for char in text:
        if char.isdigit():
            digit_count += 1
        elif char.isupper():
            uppercase_count += 1
        elif char.islower():
            lowercase_count += 1
    return {
        "digits": digit_count,
        "uppercase": uppercase_count,
        "lowercase": lowercase_count
    }

# Generate a random string
random_string = generate_random_string(10)
```

```
# Count the digits, uppercase letters, and lowercase
letters
counts = count_digits_uppercase_lowercase(random_string)

# Print the results
print("Random string:", random_string)
print("Digits:", counts["digits"])
print("Uppercase letters:", counts["uppercase"])
print("Lowercase letters:", counts["lowercase"])

"""
Explanation:
    Import Libraries:
        random library is used to generate random
characters.
        string library provides access to predefined sets of
characters like alphanumeric characters.

    Functions:
        generate_random_string:
            This function takes a length as input and
generates a random string of that length.
            It uses string.ascii_letters and string.digits
to get all uppercase, lowercase letters, and digits.
            It then uses a loop and random.choice to
randomly select characters and join them into a string.
        count_digits_uppercase_lowercase:
            This function takes a text as input and returns
a dictionary with counts for digits, uppercase, and
lowercase letters.
            It uses three counters initialized to 0: digit_
count, uppercase_count, and lowercase_count.
            It iterates through each character in the text
string.
            For each character, it uses char.isdigit(),
char.isupper(), and char.islower() methods to check its
type and increment the corresponding counter.
            Finally, it returns a dictionary with the
counts for each character type.

    Code Execution:
        generate_random_string is called with a length of
10 to create a random string.
        count_digits_uppercase_lowercase is called with the
generated string to count characters.
        Finally, the results are printed, including the
original string and counts for each character type.
Bard may display inaccurate info, including about people,
so double-check its responses.
```

Launch the code in Listing 3.11, and you will see output that is similar to the following output (which depends on the specific string):

```
Random string: fM7albOKmS
Digits: 1
```

```
Uppercase letters: 4
Lowercase letters: 5
```

Bard Python Code for a Queue

The code sample that Bard generated in this section is based on the following prompt:

```
Please generate Python code for a queue that involves a
random set of numbers, along with an explanation of the
Python code.
```

Listing 3.12 displays the content of bard_queue.py that contains Python code for a queue data structure.

LISTING 3.12: bard_queue.py

```python
import random

class RandomNumberQueue:
  def __init__(self, max_size):
    self.queue = []
    self.max_size = max_size

  def enqueue(self, number):
    if len(self.queue) >= self.max_size:
      raise OverflowError("Queue is full!")
    self.queue.append(number)

  def dequeue(self):
    if len(self.queue) == 0:
      raise ValueError("Queue is empty!")
    return self.queue.pop(0)

  def is_empty(self):
    return len(self.queue) == 0

  def size(self):
    return len(self.queue)

  def generate_random_numbers(self, n):
    for _ in range(n):
      self.enqueue(random.randint(1, 100))

  def __str__(self):
    return str(self.queue)

# Example usage
queue = RandomNumberQueue(5)
```

```
# Generate 3 random numbers and enqueue them
queue.generate_random_numbers(3)

print("Queue after enqueue:", queue)

# Dequeue one element and check if the queue is empty
dequeued_element = queue.dequeue()
print("Queue is empty:", queue.is_empty())

print("Queue after dequeue:", queue)
print("Queue size:", queue.size())

"""
Explanation:
    RandomNumberQueue class:
        This class defines a queue data structure that can
hold a random set of numbers.
        The __init__ method initializes the queue with a
specified maximum size.
        The enqueue method adds an element to the back of
the queue, checking for overflow.
        The dequeue method removes and returns the element
from the front of the queue, checking for underflow.
        The is_empty method returns True if the queue is
empty and False otherwise.
        The size method returns the number of elements in
the queue.
        The generate_random_numbers method enqueues a
specified number of random integers to the queue.
        The __str__ method returns a string representation
of the queue.

    Example usage:
        This code creates an instance of the
RandomNumberQueue class with a maximum size of 5.
        It then generates 3 random numbers and enqueues
them to the queue.
        The script dequeues one element and checks if the queue
is empty, demonstrating the dequeue and is_empty methods.
        Finally, it prints the remaining contents of the
queue and checks its size.

Bard may display inaccurate info, including about people,
so double-check its responses.
"""
```

Launch the code in Listing 3.12, and you will see output that is similar to the following output (which depends on the randomly generated numbers):

```
Queue after enqueue: [1, 39, 28]
Dequeued element: 1
Queue is empty: False
Queue after dequeue: [39, 28]
Queue size: 2
```

Bard Python Code for a Stack

The code sample that Bard generated in this section is based on the following prompt for Bard:

Please generate Python code for a stack that involves a random set of numbers, along with an explanation of the Python code.

Listing 3.13 displays the content of bard_stack.py that contains Python code for a queue data structure.

LISTING 3.13: bard_stack.py

```python
import random

class RandomNumberStack:
    def __init__(self, size):
        self.stack = []
        self.size = size

    def push(self, number):
        if len(self.stack) >= self.size:
            raise OverflowError("Stack is full!")
        self.stack.append(number)

    def pop(self):
        if len(self.stack) == 0:
            raise ValueError("Stack is empty!")
        return self.stack.pop()

    def peek(self):
        if len(self.stack) == 0:
            raise ValueError("Stack is empty!")
        return self.stack[-1]

    def is_empty(self):
        return len(self.stack) == 0

    #def size(self):
    def stack_size(self):
        return len(self.stack)

    def generate_random_numbers(self, n):
        for _ in range(n):
            self.push(random.randint(1, 100))

    def __str__(self):
        return str(self.stack)

# Example usage
stack = RandomNumberStack(5)
```

```
# Generate 3 random numbers and push them to the stack
stack.generate_random_numbers(3)
print("Stack after pushing:", stack)

# Pop and peek at the top element
popped_element = stack.pop()
peeked_element = stack.peek()

print("Popped element:", popped_element)
print("Peeked element:", peeked_element)

print("Stack after popping:", stack)
print("Is stack empty:", stack.is_empty())
#print("Stack size:", stack.size())
print("Stack size:", stack.stack_size())


"""
Explanation:
    RandomNumberStack class:
        This class defines a stack data structure that can
hold a random set of numbers.
        The __init__ method initializes the stack with a
specified size.
        The push method adds an element to the top of the
stack, checking for overflow.
        The pop method removes and returns the element from
the top of the stack, checking for underflow.
        The peek method returns the element at the top of
the stack without removing it.
        The is_empty method returns True if the stack is
empty and False otherwise.
        The size method returns the number of elements in
the stack.
        The generate_random_numbers method pushes a
specified number of random integers to the stack.
        The __str__ method returns a string representation
of the stack.

    Example usage:
        This code creates an instance of the
RandomNumberStack class with a size of 5.
        It then generates 3 random numbers and pushes them
to the stack.
        The script pops one element and peeks at the top
element, demonstrating the pop and peek methods.
        Finally, it prints the remaining contents of the
stack, checks if it's empty, and checks its size.
"""
```

Launch the code in Listing 3.13, and you will see output that is similar to the following output (which depends on the randomly generated numbers):

```
Stack after pushing: [34, 30, 70]
Popped element: 70
```

```
Peeked element: 30
Stack after popping: [34, 30]
Is stack empty: False
Stack size: 2
```

SUMMARY

This chapter showed you how to work with various Python data structures. In particular, you learned about tuples, sets, and dictionaries. Next, you learned how to work with lists and how to use list-related operations to extract sublists. In addition, you learned how to work with Bard to write Python code.

## CHAPTER 4

INTRODUCTION TO NUMPY AND PANDAS

The first half of this chapter starts with an introduction to the Python NumPy package, followed by a quick introduction to Pandas and some of its useful features. The Pandas package for Python provides a rich and powerful set of APIs for managing datasets. These APIs are very useful for machine learning and deep learning tasks that involve dynamically "slicing and dicing" subsets of datasets.

The first section contains examples of working arrays in NumPy and contrasts some of the APIs for lists with the same APIs for arrays. In addition, you will see how easy it is to compute the exponent-related values (such as squares and cubes) of elements in an array.

The second section introduces subranges, which are very useful (and frequently used) for extracting portions of datasets in machine learning tasks. You will see code samples that handle negative (−1) subranges for vectors as well as for arrays, because they are interpreted one way for vectors and a different way for arrays.

The third part of this chapter delves into other NumPy methods, including the `reshape()` method, which is extremely useful (and very common) when working with image files: some TensorFlow APIs require converting a 2D array of (R,G,B) values into a corresponding one-dimensional vector.

The fourth part of this chapter briefly describes Pandas and some of its useful features. This section contains code samples that illustrate some nice features of data frames and a brief discussion of series, which are two of the main features of Pandas. The second part of this chapter discusses various types of data frames that you can create, such as numeric and Boolean data frames. In addition, you will see examples of creating data frames with NumPy functions and random numbers.

The fifth section of this chapter shows you how to manipulate the contents of data frames with various operations. In particular, you will see code samples that illustrate how to create Pandas data frames from CSV files, Excel spreadsheets, and data that is retrieved from a URL. Finally, this chapter gives you an overview of important data cleaning tasks that you can perform with Pandas APIs.

WHAT IS NUMPY?

NumPy is a Python module that encompasses many useful methods and can improve your code's performance. NumPy provides a core library for scientific computing in Python, with performant multi-dimensional arrays and good vectorized math functions, along with support for linear algebra and random numbers.

NumPy is modeled after MATLAB, with support for lists, arrays, and so forth. NumPy is easier to use than MATLAB, and it is common in TensorFlow code as well as Python code.

Useful NumPy Features

The NumPy package contains the *ndarray* object that encapsulates multi-dimensional arrays of homogeneous data types. Many ndarray operations are performed in compiled code to improve performance.

Keep in mind the following important differences between NumPy arrays and the standard Python sequences:

- NumPy arrays have a fixed size, whereas Python lists can expand dynamically. Whenever you modify the size of ndarray, a new array is created, and the original array is deleted.
- NumPy arrays are homogeneous, which means that the elements in a NumPy array must have the same data type. Except for NumPy arrays of objects, the elements in NumPy arrays of any other data type must be the same size in memory.
- NumPy arrays support more efficient execution (and require less code) of various types of operations on large numbers of data.
- Many scientific Python-based packages rely on NumPy arrays, and knowledge of NumPy arrays is becoming increasingly important.

Now that you have a general idea about NumPy, let's delve into some examples that illustrate how to work with NumPy arrays, which is the topic of the next section.

WHAT ARE NUMPY ARRAYS?

An *array* is a set of consecutive memory locations used to store data. Each item in the array is called an *element*. The number of elements in an array is called the *dimension* of the array. A typical array declaration is shown here:

```
arr1 = np.array([1,2,3,4,5])
```

The preceding code snippet declares arr1 as an array of five elements, which you can access via arr1[0] through arr1[4]. Notice that the first element has an index value of 0, the second element has an index value of 1, and so forth. Thus, if you declare an array of 100 elements, then the 100th element has an index value of 99.

NOTE   *The first position in a NumPy* `array` *has an index of 0.*

NumPy treats arrays as vectors: Math operations are performed element-by-element. Remember the following difference: "doubling" an array *multiplies* each element by 2, whereas "doubling" a list *appends* a list to itself.

Listing 4.1 displays the content of `nparray1.py` that illustrates some operations on a NumPy array.

LISTING 4.1: nparray1.py

```
import numpy as np

list1 = [1,2,3,4,5]
print(list1)

arr1  = np.array([1,2,3,4,5])
print(arr1)

list2 = [(1,2,3),(4,5,6)]
print(list2)

arr2  = np.array([(1,2,3),(4,5,6)])
print(arr2)
```

Listing 4.1 defines the variables `list1` and `list2` (which are Python lists), as well as the variables `arr1` and `arr2` (which are arrays) and prints their values. The output from launching Listing 4.1 is here:

```
[1, 2, 3, 4, 5]
[1 2 3 4 5]
[(1, 2, 3), (4, 5, 6)]
[[1 2 3]
 [4 5 6]]
```

As you can see, Python lists and arrays are easy to define. Now we are ready to look at some loop operations for lists and arrays.

WORKING WITH LOOPS

Listing 4.2 displays the content of `loop1.py` that illustrates how to iterate through the elements of a NumPy array and a Python list.

LISTING 4.2: loop1.py

```
import numpy as np

list = [1,2,3]
arr1 = np.array([1,2,3])
```

```
for e in list:
  print(e)

for e in arr1:
  print(e)

list1 = [1,2,3,4,5]
```

Listing 4.2 initializes the variable list, which is a Python list, and also the variable arr1, which is a NumPy array. The next portion of Listing 4.2 contains two loops, each of which iterates through the elements in list and arr1. As you can see, the syntax is identical in both loops. The output from launching Listing 4.2 is here:

```
1
2
3
1
2
3
```

APPENDING ELEMENTS TO ARRAYS (1)

Listing 4.3 displays the content of append1.py that illustrates how to append elements to a NumPy array and a Python list.

LISTING 4.3: append1.py

```
import numpy as np

arr1 = np.array([1,2,3])

# these do not work:
#arr1.append(4)
#arr1 = arr1 + [5]

arr1 = np.append(arr1,4)
arr1 = np.append(arr1,[5])

for e in arr1:
  print(e)

arr2 = arr1 + arr1

for e in arr2:
  print(e)
```

Listing 4.3 initializes the variable list, which is a Python list, and also the variable arr1, which is a NumPy array. The output from launching Listing 4.3 is here:

```
1
2
3
4
5
2
4
6
8
10
```

APPENDING ELEMENTS TO ARRAYS (2)

Listing 4.4 displays the content of `append2.py` that illustrates how to append elements to a NumPy array and a Python list.

LISTING 4.4: append2.py

```python
import numpy as np

arr1 = np.array([1,2,3])
arr1 = np.append(arr1,4)

for e in arr1:
  print(e)

arr1 = np.array([1,2,3])
arr1 = np.append(arr1,4)

arr2 = arr1 + arr1

for e in arr2:
  print(e)
```

Listing 4.4 initializes the variable `arr1`, which is a NumPy array. Notice that NumPy arrays do not have an "append" method: this method is available through NumPy itself. Another important difference between Python lists and NumPy arrays is the "+" operator *concatenates* Python lists, whereas this operator *doubles* the elements in a NumPy array. The output from launching Listing 4.4 is here:

```
1
2
3
4
2
4
6
8
```

MULTIPLY LISTS AND ARRAYS

Listing 4.5 displays the content of `multiply1.py` that illustrates how to multiply elements in a Python list and a NumPy array.

LISTING 4.5: multiply1.py

```
import numpy as np

list1 = [1,2,3]
arr1 = np.array([1,2,3])
print('list:  ',list1)
print('arr1:  ',arr1)
print('2*list:',2*list)
print('2*arr1:',2*arr1)
```

Listing 4.5 contains a Python list called `list` and a NumPy array called `arr1`. The `print()` statements display the contents of `list` and `arr1`, as well as the result of doubling `list1` and `arr1`. Recall that "doubling" a Python list is different from doubling a Python array, which you can see in the output from launching Listing 4.5:

```
('list:  ', [1, 2, 3])
('arr1:  ', array([1, 2, 3]))
('2*list:', [1, 2, 3, 1, 2, 3])
('2*arr1:', array([2, 4, 6]))
```

DOUBLING THE ELEMENTS IN A LIST

Listing 4.6 displays the content of `double_list1.py` that illustrates how to double the elements in a Python list.

LISTING 4.6: double_list1.py

```
import numpy as np

list1 = [1,2,3]
list2 = []

for e in list1:
  list2.append(2*e)

print('list1:',list1)
print('list2:',list2)
```

Listing 4.6 contains a Python list called `list1` and an empty NumPy list called `list2`. The next code snippet iterates through the elements of `list1` and appends them to the variable `list2`. The pair of `print()` statements display the contents of `list1` and `list2` to show you that they are the same. The output from launching Listing 4.6 is here:

```
('list:  ', [1, 2, 3])
('list2:', [2, 4, 6])
```

LISTS AND EXPONENTS

Listing 4.7 displays the content of `exponent_list1.py` that illustrates how to compute exponents of the elements in a Python list.

LISTING 4.7: exponent_list1.py

```
import numpy as np

list1 = [1,2,3]
list2 = []

for e in list1:
  list2.append(e*e) # e*e = squared

print('list1:',list1)
print('list2:',list2)
```

Listing 4.7 contains a Python list called list1 and an empty NumPy list called list2. The next code snippet iterates through the elements of list1 and appends the square of each element to the variable list2. The pair of print() statements display the contents of list1 and list2. The output from launching Listing 4.7 is here:

```
('list1:', [1, 2, 3])
('list2:', [1, 4, 9])
```

ARRAYS AND EXPONENTS

Listing 4.8 displays the content of exponent_array1.py that illustrates how to compute exponents of the elements in a NumPy array.

LISTING 4.8: exponent_array1.py

```
import numpy as np

arr1 = np.array([1,2,3])
arr2 = arr1**2
arr3 = arr1**3

print('arr1:',arr1)
print('arr2:',arr2)
print('arr3:',arr3)
```

Listing 4.8 contains a NumPy array called arr1, followed by two NumPy arrays called arr2 and arr3. Notice the compact manner in which arr2 is initialized with the square of the elements in arr1, followed by the initialization of the array arr3 with the cube of the elements in arr1. The three print() statements display the contents of arr1, arr2, and arr3. The output from launching Listing 4.8 is here:

```
('arr1:', array([1, 2, 3]))
('arr2:', array([1, 4, 9]))
('arr3:', array([ 1,  8, 27]))
```

MATH OPERATIONS AND ARRAYS

Listing 4.9 displays the content of `mathops_array1.py` that illustrates how to compute exponents of the elements in a NumPy array.

LISTING 4.9: mathops_array1.py

```
import numpy as np

arr1 = np.array([1,2,3])
sqrt = np.sqrt(arr1)
log1 = np.log(arr1)
exp1 = np.exp(arr1)

print('sqrt:',sqrt)
print('log1:',log1)
print('exp1:',exp1)
```

Listing 4.9 contains an array called `arr1`, followed by three arrays called `sqrt`, `log1`, and `exp1` that are initialized with the square root, log, and exponential value of the elements in `arr1`, respectively. The three `print()` statements display the contents of `sqrt`, `log1`, and `exp1`. The output from launching Listing 4.9 is here:

```
('sqrt:', array([1.        , 1.41421356, 1.73205081]))
('log1:', array([0.        , 0.69314718, 1.09861229]))
('exp1:', array([2.71828183, 7.3890561,  20.08553692]))
```

WORKING WITH "−1" SUBRANGES WITH VECTORS

Listing 4.10 displays the content of `npsubarray2.py` that illustrates how to compute exponents of the elements in a NumPy array.

LISTING 4.10: npsubarray2.py

```
import numpy as np

# -1 => "all except the last element in …" (row or col)

arr1  = np.array([1,2,3,4,5])
print('arr1:',arr1)
print('arr1[0:-1]:',arr1[0:-1])
print('arr1[1:-1]:',arr1[1:-1])
print('arr1[::-1]:', arr1[::-1]) # reverse!
```

Listing 4.10 contains an array called `arr1`, followed by four `print()` statements, each of which displays a different subrange of values in `arr1`. The output from launching Listing 4.10 is here:

```
('arr1:',        array([1, 2, 3, 4, 5]))
('arr1[0:-1]:', array([1, 2, 3, 4]))
```

```
('arr1[1:-1]:', array([2, 3, 4]))
('arr1[::-1]:', array([5, 4, 3, 2, 1]))
```

WORKING WITH "–1" SUBRANGES WITH ARRAYS

Listing 4.11 displays the content of np2darray2.py that illustrates how to compute exponents of the elements in a NumPy array.

LISTING 4.11: np2darray2.py

```
import numpy as np

# -1 => "the last element in ..." (row or col)

arr1  = np.array([[(1,2,3),(4,5,6),(7,8,9),(10,11,12)])
print('arr1:',          arr1)
print('arr1[-1,:]:',   arr1[-1,:])
print('arr1[:,-1]:',   arr1[:,-1])
print('arr1[-1:,-1]:',arr1[-1:,-1])
```

Listing 4.11 contains an array called arr1, followed by four print() statements, each of which displays a different subrange of values in arr1. The output from launching Listing 4.11 is here:

```
(arr1:', array([[1,    2,    3],
                [4,    5,    6],
                [7,    8,    9],
                [10, 11, 12]]))
(arr1[-1,:]]',    array([10, 11, 12]))
(arr1[:,-1]:',    array([3,    6,    9, 12]))
(arr1[-1:,-1]]', array([12]))
```

OTHER USEFUL NUMPY METHODS

In addition to the NumPy methods that you saw in the code samples prior to this section, the following (often intuitively-named) methods are also very useful.

- The method np.zeros() initializes an array with 0 values.
- The method np.ones() initializes an array with 1 value.
- The method np.empty() initializes an array with 0 values.
- The method np.arange() provides a range of numbers:
- The method np.shape() displays the shape of an object:
- The method np.reshape() <= *very useful!*
- The method np.linspace() <= *useful in regression*
- The method np.mean() computes the mean of a set of numbers.
- The method np.std() computes the standard deviation of a set of numbers.

Although `np.zeros()` and `np.empty()` both initialize a 2D array with 0, `np.zeros()` requireslessexecutiontime.Youcouldalsousenp.`full(size,0)`, but this method is the slowest of all three methods.

The `reshape()` and `linspace()` methods are useful for changing the dimensions of an array and generating a list of numeric values, respectively. The `reshape()` method often appears in TensorFlow code, and the `linspace()` method is useful for generating a set of numbers in linear regressions.

The `mean()` and `std()` methods are useful for calculating the mean and the standard deviation of a set of numbers. For example, you can use these two methods to resize the values in a Gaussian distribution so that their mean is 0 and the standard deviation is 1. This process is called *standardizing* a Gaussian distribution.

ARRAYS AND VECTOR OPERATIONS

Listing 4.12 displays the content of `array_vector.py` that illustrates how to perform vector operations on the elements in a NumPy array.

LISTING 4.12: array_vector.py

```
import numpy as np

a = np.array([[1,2], [3, 4]])
b = np.array([[5,6], [7,8]])

print('a:         ', a)
print('b:         ', b)
print('a + b:     ', a+b)
print('a - b:     ', a-b)
print('a * b:     ', a*b)
print('a / b:     ', a/b)
print('b / a:     ', b/a)
print('a.dot(b):',a.dot(b))
```

Listing 4.12 contains two arrays called a and b, followed by eight `print()` statements, each of which displays the result of "applying" a different arithmetic operation to the arrays a and b. The output from launching Listing 4.12 is here:

```
('a    :   ', array([[1, 2], [3, 4]]))
('b    :   ', array([[5, 6], [7, 8]]))
('a + b:   ', array([[ 6,  8], [10, 12]]))
('a - b:   ', array([[-4, -4], [-4, -4]]))
('a * b:   ', array([[ 5, 12], [21, 32]]))
('a / b:   ', array([[0, 0], [0, 0]]))
('b / a:   ', array([[5, 3], [2, 2]]))
('a.dot(b):', array([[19, 22], [43, 50]]))
```

NUMPY AND DOT PRODUCTS (1)

Listing 4.13 displays the content of `dotproduct1.py` that illustrates how to perform the dot product on the elements in a NumPy array.

LISTING 4.13: dotproduct1.py

```
import numpy as np

a = np.array([1,2])
b = np.array([2,3])

dot2 = 0
for e,f in zip(a,b):
  dot2 += e*f

print('a:    ',a)
print('b:    ',b)
print('a*b: ',a*b)
print('dot1:',a.dot(b))
print('dot2:',dot2)
```

Listing 4.13 contains two arrays called a and b, followed by a simple loop that computes the dot product of a and b. The next section contains five `print()` statements that display the contents of a and b, their inner product that is calculated in three different ways. The output from launching Listing 4.13 is here:

```
('a:    ', array([1, 2]))
('b:    ', array([2, 3]))
('a*b: ', array([2, 6]))
('dot1:', 8)
('dot2:', 8)
```

NUMPY AND DOT PRODUCTS (2)

NumPy arrays support a "dot" method for calculating the inner product of an array of numbers, which uses the same formula that you use for calculating the inner product of a pair of vectors. Listing 4.14 displays the content of `dotproduct2.py` that illustrates how to calculate the dot product of two NumPy arrays.

LISTING 4.14: dotproduct2.py

```
import numpy as np

a = np.array([1,2])
b = np.array([2,3])
```

```
print('a:             ',a)
print('b:             ',b)
print('a.dot(b):     ',a.dot(b))
print('b.dot(a):     ',b.dot(a))
print('np.dot(a,b):',np.dot(a,b))
print('np.dot(b,a):',np.dot(b,a))
```

Listing 4.14 contains two arrays called a and b, followed by six print() statements that display the contents of a and b, as well as their inner product that is calculated in three different ways. The output from launching Listing 4.14 is here:

```
('a:             ', array([1, 2]))
('b:             ', array([2, 3]))
('a.dot(b):     ', 8)
('b.dot(a):     ', 8)
('np.dot(a,b):', 8)
('np.dot(b,a):', 8)
```

NUMPY AND THE "NORM" OF VECTORS

The "norm" of a vector (or an array of numbers) is the length of a vector, which is the square root of the dot product of a vector with itself. NumPy also provides the "sum" and "square" functions that you can use to calculate the norm of a vector.

Listing 4.15 displays the content of array_norm.py that illustrates how to calculate the magnitude ("norm") of a NumPy array of numbers.

LISTING 4.15: array_norm.py

```
import numpy as np

a = np.array([2,3])
asquare = np.square(a)
asqsum  = np.sum(np.square(a))
anorm1  = np.sqrt(np.sum(a*a))
anorm2  = np.sqrt(np.sum(np.square(a)))
anorm3  = np.linalg.norm(a)

print('a:        ',a)
print('asquare:',asquare)
print('asqsum:  ',asqsum)
print('anorm1:  ',anorm1)
print('anorm2:  ',anorm2)
print('anorm3:  ',anorm3)
```

Listing 4.15 contains an initial array called a, followed by the array asquare and the numeric values asqsum, anorm1, anorm2, and anorm3. The array asquare contains the square of the elements in array a, and the numeric value asqsum contains the sum of the elements in the array asquare.

Next, the numeric value `anorm1` equals the square root of the sum of the square of the elements in a. The numeric value `anorm2` is the same as `anorm1`, computed in a slightly different fashion. Finally, the numeric value `anorm3` is equal to `anorm2`, but as you can see, `anorm3` is calculated via a single NumPy method, whereas `anorm2` requires a succession of NumPy methods.

The last portion of Listing 4.15 consists of six `print()` statements, each of which displays the computed values. The output from launching Listing 4.15 is here:

```
('a:         ', array([2, 3]))
('asquare:', array([4, 9]))
('asqsum: ', 13)
('anorm1: ', 3.605551275463989)
('anorm2: ', 3.605551275463989)
('anorm3: ', 3.605551275463989)
```

NUMPY AND OTHER OPERATIONS

NumPy provides the "*" operator to multiply the components of two vectors to produce a third vector, whose components are the products of the corresponding components of the initial pair of vectors. This operation is called a Hadamard product, which is named after a famous mathematician. If you then add the components of the third vector, the sum is equal to the inner product of the initial pair of vectors.

Listing 4.16 displays the content of `otherops.py` that illustrates how to perform other operations on a NumPy array.

LISTING 4.16: otherops.py

```
import numpy as np

a = np.array([1,2])
b = np.array([3,4])

print('a:          ',a)
print('b:          ',b)
print('a*b:        ',a*b)
print('np.sum(a*b): ',np.sum(a*b))
print('(a*b.sum()): ',(a*b).sum())
```

Listing 4.16 contains two arrays called a and b, followed five `print()` statements that display the contents of a and b, their Hadamard product, and their inner product that is calculated in two different ways. The output from launching Listing 4.16 is here:

```
('a:          ', array([1, 2]))
('b:          ', array([3, 4]))
('a*b:        ', array([3, 8]))
('np.sum(a*b): ', 11)
('(a*b.sum()): ', 11)
```

NUMPY AND THE RESHAPE() METHOD

NumPy arrays support the `reshape()` method, which enables you to restructure the dimensions of an array of numbers. In general, if a NumPy array contains m elements, where m is a positive integer, then that array can be restructured as an m1 x m2 array, where m1 and m2 are positive integers such that m1*m2 = m.

Listing 4.17 displays the content of `numpy_reshape.py` that illustrates how to use the `reshape()` method on a NumPy array.

LISTING 4.17: numpy_reshape.py

```
import numpy as np

x = np.array([[2, 3], [4, 5], [6, 7]])
print(x.shape)  # (3, 2)

x = x.reshape((2, 3))
print(x.shape)  # (2, 3)
print('x1:',x)

x = x.reshape((-1))
print(x.shape)  # (6,)
print('x2:',x)

x = x.reshape((6, -1))
print(x.shape)  # (6, 1)
print('x3:',x)

x = x.reshape((-1, 6))
print(x.shape)  # (1, 6)
print('x4:',x)
```

Listing 4.17 contains an array called x, whose dimensions are 3x2, followed by a set of invocations of the `reshape()` method that reshape the contents of x. The first invocation of the `reshape()` method changes the shape of x from 3x2 to 2x3. The second invocation changes the shape of x from 2x3 to 6x1. The third invocation changes the shape of x from 1x6 to 6x1. The final invocation changes the shape of x from 6x1 to 1x6 again.

Each invocation of the `reshape()` method is followed by a `print()` statement so that you can see the effect of the invocation. The output from launching Listing 4.17 is here:

```
(3, 2)
(2, 3)
('x1:', array([[2, 3, 4],
       [5, 6, 7]]))
(6,)
('x2:', array([2, 3, 4, 5, 6, 7]))
(6, 1)
```

```
('x3:', array([[2],
        [3],
        [4],
        [5],
        [6],
        [7]]))
(1, 6)
```

CALCULATING THE MEAN AND STANDARD DEVIATION

If you need to review these concepts from statistics (and perhaps also the mean, median, and mode), please read the appropriate on-line tutorials.

NumPy provides various built-in functions that perform statistical calculations, such as the following list of methods:

```
np.linspace() <= useful for regression
np.mean()
np.std()
```

The np.linspace() method generates a set of equally spaced numbers between a lower bound and an upper bound. The np.mean() and np.std() methods calculate the mean and standard deviation, respectively, of a set of numbers. Listing 4.18 displays the content of sample_mean_std.py that illustrates how to calculate statistical values from a NumPy array.

LISTING 4.18: sample_mean_std.py

```
import numpy as np

x2 = np.arange(8)
print('mean = ',x2.mean())
print('std = ',x2.std())

x3 = (x2 - x2.mean())/x2.std()
print('x3 mean = ',x3.mean())
print('x3 std = ',x3.std())
```

Listing 4.18 contains the array x2 that consists of the first eight integers. Next, mean() and std(), which are "associated" with x2, are invoked to calculate the mean and standard deviation, respectively, of the elements of x2. The output from launching Listing 4.18 is here:

```
('a:           ', array([1, 2]))
('b:           ', array([3, 4]))
```

CALCULATING QUARTILES WITH NUMPY

The code sample in this section extends the code sample in the previous section with additional statistical values, and the code in Listing 4.19 can be used for any data distribution. Keep in mind that the code sample uses random numbers simply for the purposes of illustration: after you have launched the code sample, replace those numbers with values from a CSV file or some other dataset containing meaningful values.

Moreover, this section does not provide details regarding the meaning of quartiles, but you can learn about quartiles at *https://en.wikipedia.org/wiki/ Quartile*.

Listing 4.19 displays the content of `stat_summary.py` that illustrates how to display various statistical values from a NumPy array of random numbers.

LISTING 4.19: stat_values.py

```
import numpy as np

from numpy import percentile
from numpy.random import rand

# generate data sample
data = np.random.rand(1000)

# calculate quartiles, min, and max
quartiles = percentile(data, [25, 50, 75])
data_min, data_max = data.min(), data.max()

# print summary information
print('Minimum:   %.3f' % data_min)
print('Q1 value: %.3f' % quartiles[0])
print('Median:    %.3f' % quartiles[1])
print('Mean Val: %.3f' % data.mean())
print('Std Dev:   %.3f' % data.std())
print('Q3 value: %.3f' % quartiles[2])
print('Maximum:   %.3f' % data_max)
```

The data sample (shown in bold) in Listing 4.19 is from a uniform distribution between 0 and 1. The `percentile()` function calculates a linear interpolation (average) between observations, which is needed to calculate the median on a sample with an even number of values. As you can surmise, the functions `min()` and `max()` calculate the smallest and largest values in the data sample. The output from launching Listing 4.19 is here:

```
Minimum:   0.000
Q1 value: 0.237
Median:    0.500
Mean Val: 0.495
Std Dev:   0.295
Q3 value: 0.747
Maximum:   0.999
```

This concludes the portion of the chapter pertaining to NumPy. The second half of this chapter discusses some of the features of Pandas.

WHAT IS PANDAS?

Pandas is a Python package that is compatible with other Python packages, such as NumPy and Matplotlib. Install Pandas by opening a command shell and invoking this command for Python 3.x:

```
pip3 install pandas
```

In many ways the Pandas package has the semantics of a spreadsheet, and it also works with XSL, XML, HTML, and CSV file types. Pandas has a data type called DataFrame (similar to a Python dictionary) with an extremely powerful functionality, which is discussed in the next section.

Pandas DataFrames support a variety of input types, such as `ndarrays`, lists, `dicts`, and `Series`. Pandas also has another data type called `Pandas Series` (not discussed in this chapter); this data structure provides another mechanism for managing data (search online for more details).

Pandas Data Frames

In simplified terms, a Pandas DataFrame is a two-dimensional data structure, and it is convenient to think of the data structure in terms of rows and columns. DataFrames can be labeled (rows as well as columns), and the columns can contain different data types.

By way of analogy, it might be useful to think of a DataFrame as the counterpart to a spreadsheet, which makes it a very useful data type in Pandas-related Python scripts. The source of the dataset can be a data file, database tables, Web service, and so forth. Pandas data frame features include the following:

- DataFrame Methods
- DataFrame Statistics
- Grouping, Pivoting, and Reshaping
- Dealing with Missing Data
- Joining DataFrames

DataFrames and Data Cleaning Tasks

The specific tasks that you need to perform depend on the structure and contents of a dataset. In general, you will perform a workflow with the following steps (not necessarily always in this order), all of which can be performed with a Pandas DataFrame:

- Read data into a DataFrame
- Display the top of a DataFrame
- Display column data types
- Display non-missing values
- Replace NA with a value
- Iterate through the columns
- Statistics for each column

- Find missing values
- Total missing values
- Percentage of missing values
- Sort table values
- Print summary information
- Columns with > 50% missing
- Rename columns

A LABELED PANDAS DATAFRAME

Listing 4.20 displays the content of `pandas_labeled_df.py` that illustrates how to define a DataFrame whose rows and columns are labeled.

LISTING 4.20: pandas_labeled_df.py

```
import numpy
import pandas

myarray = numpy.array([[10,30,20],
[50,40,60],[1000,2000,3000]])

rownames = ['apples', 'oranges', 'beer']
colnames = ['January', 'February', 'March']

mydf = Pandas.DataFrame(myarray, index=rownames,
columns=colnames)

print(mydf)
print(mydf.describe())
```

Listing 4.20 contains two important statements followed by the variable `myarray`, which is a 3x3 NumPy array of numbers. The variables `rownames` and `colnames` provide names for the rows and columns, respectively, of the data in `myarray`. Next, the variable `mydf` is initialized as a DataFrame with the specified data source (i.e., `myarray`).

You might be surprised to see that the first portion of the output below requires a single `print()` statement (which simply displays the contents of `mydf`). The second portion of the output is generated by invoking the `describe()` method that is available for any NumPy DataFrame. The `describe()` method is very useful: you will see various statistical quantities, such as the mean, standard deviation minimum, and maximum performed `column_wise` (not `row_wise`), along with values for the 25th, 50th, and 75th percentiles. The output of Listing 4.20 is here:

```
        January  February  March
apples       10        30     20
oranges      50        40     60
beer       1000      2000   3000
```

```
            January      February        March
count      3.000000      3.000000     3.000000
mean     353.333333    690.000000  1026.666667
std      560.386771   1134.504297  1709.073823
min       10.000000     30.000000    20.000000
25%       30.000000     35.000000    40.000000
50%       50.000000     40.000000    60.000000
75%      525.000000   1020.000000  1530.000000
max     1000.000000   2000.000000  3000.000000
```

PANDAS NUMERIC DATAFRAMES

Listing 4.21 displays the content of `pandas_numeric_df.py` that illustrates how to define a DataFrame whose rows and columns are numbers (but the column labels are characters).

LISTING 4.21: pandas_numeric_df.py

```
import pandas as pd

df1 = pd.DataFrame(np.random.randn(10, 4),columns=['A','B','C','D'])
df2 = pd.DataFrame(np.random.randn(7, 3), columns=['A','B','C'])
df3 = df1 + df2
```

The essence of Listing 4.21 involves initializing the DataFrames `df1` and `df2`, and then defining the DataFrame `df3` as the sum of `df1` and `df2`. The output from Listing 4.21 is here:

```
        A        B        C    D
0   0.0457  -0.0141   1.3809  NaN
1  -0.9554  -1.5010   0.0372  NaN
2  -0.6627   1.5348  -0.8597  NaN
3  -2.4529   1.2373  -0.1337  NaN
4   1.4145   1.9517  -2.3204  NaN
5  -0.4949  -1.6497  -1.0846  NaN
6  -1.0476  -0.7486  -0.8055  NaN
7      NaN      NaN      NaN  NaN
8      NaN      NaN      NaN  NaN
9      NaN      NaN      NaN  NaN
```

Keep in mind that the default behavior for operations involving a `DataFrame` and `Series` is to align the `Series` index on the `DataFrame` columns; this results in a row-wise output. Here is a simple illustration:

```
names = pd.Series(['SF', 'San Jose', 'Sacramento'])
sizes = pd.Series([852469, 1015785, 485199])

df = pd.DataFrame({ 'Cities': names, 'Size': sizes })
df = pd.DataFrame({ 'City name': names,'sizes': sizes })

print(df)
```

The output of the preceding code block is here:

```
   City name     sizes
0         SF    852469
1   San Jose   1015785
2  Sacramento    485199
```

PANDAS BOOLEAN DATAFRAMES

Pandas supports Boolean operations on DataFrames, such as the logical or, the logical and, and the logical negation of a pair of DataFrames. Listing 4.22 displays the content of pandas_boolean_df.py that illustrates how to define a DataFrame whose rows and columns are Boolean values.

LISTING 4.22: pandas_boolean_df.py

```python
import pandas as pd

df1 = pd.DataFrame({'a' : [1, 0, 1], 'b' : [0, 1, 1] }, dtype=bool)
df2 = pd.DataFrame({'a' : [0, 1, 1], 'b' : [1, 1, 0] }, dtype=bool)

print("df1 & df2:")
print(df1 & df2)

print("df1 | df2:")
print(df1 | df2)

print("df1 ^ df2:")
print(df1 ^ df2)
```

Listing 4.22 initializes the DataFrames df1 and df2, and then computes df1 & df2, df1 | df2, df1 ^ df2, which represent the logical AND, the logical OR, and the logical negation, respectively, of df1 and df2. The output from launching the code in Listing 4.22 is here:

```
df1 & df2:
       a      b
0  False  False
1  False   True
2   True  False
df1 | df2:
      a     b
0  True  True
1  True  True
2  True  True
df1 ^ df2:
       a      b
0   True   True
1   True  False
2  False   True
```

Transposing a Pandas DataFrame

The T attribute (as well as the transpose function) enables you to generate the transpose of a Pandas DataFrame, similar to a NumPy ndarray.

For example, the following code snippet defines a Pandas DataFrame df1 and then displays the transpose of df1:

```
df1 = pd.DataFrame({'a' : [1, 0, 1], 'b' : [0, 1, 1] }, dtype=int)

print("df1.T:")
print(df1.T)
```

The output is here:

```
df1.T:
   0  1  2
a  1  0  1
b  0  1  1
```

The following code snippet defines the Pandas DataFrames df1 and df2 and then displays their sum:

```
df1 = pd.DataFrame({'a' : [1, 0, 1], 'b' : [0, 1, 1] }, dtype=int)
df2 = pd.DataFrame({'a' : [3, 3, 3], 'b' : [5, 5, 5] }, dtype=int)

print("df1 + df2:")
print(df1 + df2)
```

The output is here:

```
df1 + df2:
   a  b
0  4  5
1  3  6
2  4  6
```

PANDAS DATAFRAMES AND RANDOM NUMBERS

Listing 4.23 displays the content of pandas_random_df.py that illustrates how to create a DataFrame with random numbers.

LISTING 4.23: pandas_random_df.py

```
import pandas as pd
import numpy as np

df = pd.DataFrame(np.random.randint(1, 5, size=(5, 2)),
columns=['a','b'])
df = df.append(df.agg(['sum', 'mean']))
```

```
print("Contents of dataframe:")
print(df)
```

Listing 4.23 defines the DataFrame df, which consists of 5 rows and 2 columns of random integers between 1 and 5. Notice that the columns of df are labeled "a" and "b." In addition, the next code snippet appends two rows consisting of the sum and the mean of the numbers in both columns. The output of Listing 4.23 is here:

```
a      b
0       1.0   2.0
1       1.0   1.0
2       4.0   3.0
3       3.0   1.0
4       1.0   2.0
sum    10.0   9.0
mean    2.0   1.8
```

COMBINING PANDAS DATAFRAMES (1)

Listing 4.24 displays the content of `pandas_combine_df.py` that illustrates how to combine DataFrames.

LISTING 4.24: pandas_combine_df.py

```
import pandas as pd
import numpy as np

df = pd.DataFrame({'foo1' : np.random.randn(5),
                   'foo2' : np.random.randn(5)})

print("contents of df:")
print(df)

print("contents of foo1:")
print(df.foo1)

print("contents of foo2:")
print(df.foo2)
```

Listing 4.24 defines the DataFrame df, which consists of 5 rows and 2 columns (labeled "foo1" and "foo2") of random real numbers between 0 and 5. The next portion of Listing 4.5 displays the content of df and foo1. The output of Listing 4.24 is here:

```
contents of df:
        foo1       foo2
0   0.274680  -0.848669
1  -0.399771  -0.814679
2   0.454443  -0.363392
```

```
3   0.473753   0.550849
4  -0.211783  -0.015014
contents of foo1:
0     0.256773
1     1.204322
2     1.040515
3    -0.518414
4     0.634141
Name: foo1, dtype: float64
contents of foo2:
0    -2.506550
1    -0.896516
2    -0.222923
3     0.934574
4     0.527033
Name: foo2, dtype: float64
```

COMBINING PANDAS DATAFRAMES (2)

Pandas has the `concat()` method, which is used to concatenate DataFrames. Listing 4.25 displays the content of `concat-frames.py` that illustrates how to combine two DataFrames.

LISTING 4.25: concat_frames.py

```
import pandas as pd

can_weather = pd.DataFrame({
    "city": ["Vancouver","Toronto","Montreal"],
    "temperature": [72,65,50],
    "humidity": [40, 20, 25]
})

us_weather = pd.DataFrame({
    "city": ["SF","Chicago","LA"],
    "temperature": [60,40,85],
    "humidity": [30, 15, 55]
})

df = pd.concat([can_weather, us_weather])
print(df)
```

The first line in Listing 4.25 is an `import` statement, followed by the definition of the Pandas DataFrames `can_weather` and `us_weather` that contain weather-related information for cities in Canada and the USA, respectively. The Pandas DataFrame `df` is the concatenation of `can_weather` and `us_weather`. The output from Listing 4.25 is here:

```
0   Vancouver       40          72
1     Toronto       20          65
2    Montreal       25          50
0          SF       30          60
```

```
1     Chicago          15              40
2          LA          55              85
```

DATA MANIPULATION WITH PANDAS DATAFRAMES (1)

As a simple example, suppose that we have a two-person company that keeps track of income and expenses on a quarterly basis. We want to calculate the profit/loss for each quarter, as well as the overall profit/loss.

Listing 4.26 displays the content of `pandas_quarterly_df1.py` that illustrates how to define a Pandas DataFrame consisting of income-related values.

LISTING 4.26: pandas_quarterly_df1.py

```python
import pandas as pd

summary = {
    'Quarter': ['Q1', 'Q2', 'Q3', 'Q4'],
    'Cost':    [23500, 34000, 57000, 32000],
    'Revenue': [40000, 40000, 40000, 40000]
}

df = pd.DataFrame(summary)

print("Entire Dataset:\n",df)
print("Quarter:\n",df.Quarter)
print("Cost:\n",df.Cost)
print("Revenue:\n",df.Revenue)
```

Listing 4.26 defines the variable `summary`, which contains hard-coded quarterly information about cost and revenue for our two-person company. In general, these hard-coded values would be replaced by data from another source (such as a CSV file), so think of this code sample as a simple way to illustrate some of the functionality that is available for Pandas DataFrames.

The variable `df` is a DataFrame based on the data in the `summary` variable. The three `print()` statements display the quarters, the cost per quarter, and the revenue per quarter.

The output from Listing 4.26 is here:

```
Entire Dataset:
      Cost Quarter  Revenue
0   23500      Q1    40000
1   34000      Q2    60000
2   57000      Q3    50000
3   32000      Q4    30000
Quarter:
0     Q1
1     Q2
2     Q3
3     Q4
```

```
Name: Quarter, dtype: object
Cost:
 0    23500
 1    34000
 2    57000
 3    32000
Name: Cost, dtype: int64
Revenue:
 0    40000
 1    60000
 2    50000
 3    30000
Name: Revenue, dtype: int64
```

DATA MANIPULATION WITH PANDAS DATAFRAMES (2)

In this section, let's suppose that we have a two-person company that keeps track of income and expenses on a quarterly basis. We want to calculate the profit/loss for each quarter, as well as the overall profit/loss.

Listing 4.27 displays the content of pandas_quarterly_df1.py that illustrates how to define a DataFrame consisting of income-related values.

LISTING 4.27: pandas_quarterly_df2.py

```
import pandas as pd

summary = {
    'Quarter': ['Q1', 'Q2', 'Q3', 'Q4'],
    'Cost':    [-23500, -34000, -57000, -32000],
    'Revenue': [40000, 40000, 40000, 40000]
}

df = pd.DataFrame(summary)
print("First Dataset:\n",df)

df['Total'] = df.sum(axis=1)
print("Second Dataset:\n",df)
```

Listing 4.27 defines the variable summary, which contains quarterly information about cost and revenue for our two-person company. The variable df is a DataFrame based on the data in the summary variable. The three print() statements display the quarters, cost per quarter, and revenue per quarter. The output from Listing 4.27 is here:

```
First Dataset:
     Cost Quarter  Revenue
0 -23500      Q1    40000
1 -34000      Q2    60000
2 -57000      Q3    50000
3 -32000      Q4    30000
```

```
Second Dataset:
     Cost Quarter  Revenue   Total
0 -23500      Q1    40000   16500
1 -34000      Q2    60000   26000
2 -57000      Q3    50000   -7000
3 -32000      Q4    30000   -2000
```

DATA MANIPULATION WITH PANDAS DATAFRAMES (3)

Let's start with the same assumption as in the previous section. We have a two-person company that keeps track of income and expenses on a quarterly basis. We want to calculate the profit/loss for each quarter, as well as the overall profit/loss. In addition, we want to compute the column totals and row totals.

Listing 4.28 displays the content of pandas_quarterly_df1.py that illustrates how to define a DataFrame consisting of income-related values.

LISTING 4.28: pandas_quarterly_df3.py

```python
import pandas as pd

summary = {
    'Quarter': ['Q1', 'Q2', 'Q3', 'Q4'],
    'Cost':    [-23500, -34000, -57000, -32000],
    'Revenue': [40000, 40000, 40000, 40000]
}

df = pd.DataFrame(summary)
print("First Dataset:\n",df)

df['Total'] = df.sum(axis=1)
df.loc['Sum'] = df.sum()
print("Second Dataset:\n",df)

# or df.loc['avg'] / 3
#df.loc['avg'] = df[:3].mean()
#print("Third Dataset:\n",df)
```

Listing 4.28 defines the variable summary, which contains quarterly information about the cost and revenue for our two-person company. The variable df is a DataFrame based on the data in the summary variable. The three print() statements display the quarters, cost per quarter, and revenue per quarter. The output from Listing 4.28 is here:

```
First Dataset:
     Cost Quarter  Revenue
0 -23500      Q1    40000
1 -34000      Q2    60000
2 -57000      Q3    50000
3 -32000      Q4    30000
Second Dataset:
          Cost    Quarter  Revenue   Total
0      -23500         Q1    40000   16500
1      -34000         Q2    60000   26000
2      -57000         Q3    50000   -7000
```

```
3     -32000         Q4     30000  -2000
Sum -146500  Q1Q2Q3Q4   180000  33500
```

PANDAS DATAFRAMES AND CSV FILES

The code samples in several earlier sections contain hard-coded data inside the Python scripts. However, it is also common to read data from a CSV file. You can use the Python `csv.reader()` function, the NumPy `loadtxt()` function, or the Pandas `read_csv()` function (shown in this section) to read the contents of CSV files.

Listing 4.29 displays the content of `weather_data.py` that illustrates how to read a CSV file, initialize a DataFrame with the contents of that CSV file, and display various subsets of the data in the DataFrames.

LISTING 4.29: weather_data.py

```python
import pandas as pd

df = pd.read_csv("weather_data.csv")

print(df)
print(df.shape)   # rows, columns
print(df.head())  # df.head(3)
print(df.tail())
print(df[1:3])
print(df.columns)
print(type(df['day']))
print(df[['day','temperature']])
print(df['temperature'].max())
```

Listing 4.29 invokes the Pandas `read_csv()` function to read the contents of the CSV file `weather_data.csv`, followed by a set of Python `print()` statements that display various portions of the CSV file. The output from Listing 4.29 is here:

```
day,temperature,windspeed,event
7/1/2018,42,16,Rain
7/2/2018,45,3,Sunny
7/3/2018,78,12,Snow
7/4/2018,74,9,Snow
7/5/2018,42,24,Rain
7/6/2018,51,32,Sunny
```

In some situations, you might need to apply Boolean conditional logic to "filter out" some rows of data, based on a conditional condition that is applied to a column value.

Listing 4.30 displays the content of the CSV file `people.csv`, and Listing 4.31 displays the content of `people_pandas.py` that illustrates how to define a DataFrame that reads the CSV file and manipulates the data.

LISTING 4.30: people.csv

```
fname,lname,age,gender,country
john,smith,30,m,usa
jane,smith,31,f,france
jack,jones,32,f,france
dave,stone,33,f,france
sara,stein,34,f,france
eddy,bower,35,f,france
```

LISTING 4.31: people_pandas.py

```
import pandas as pd

df = pd.read_csv('people.csv')
df.info()
print('fname:')
print(df['fname'])
print('_____')
print('age over 33:')
print(df['age'] > 33)
print('_____')
print('age over 33:')
myfilter = df['age'] >   33
print(df[myfilter])
```

Listing 4.31 populates the DataFrame df with the contents of the CSV file people.csv. The next portion of Listing 4.12 displays the structure of df, followed by the first names of all the people. The next portion of Listing 4.12 displays a tabular list of six rows containing either True or False depending on whether a person is over 33 or at most 33, respectively.

The final portion of Listing 4.31 displays a tabular list of two rows containing all the details of the people who are over 33. The output from Listing 4.31 is here:

```
myfilter = df['age'] >   33
<class 'pandas.core.frame.DataFrame'>
RangeIndex: 6 entries, 0 to 5
Data columns (total 5 columns):
fname       6 non_null object
lname       6 non_null object
age         6 non_null int64
gender      6 non_null object
country     6 non_null object
dtypes: int64(1), object(4)
memory usage: 320.0+ bytes
fname:
0     john
1     jane
2     jack
3     dave
4     sara
5     eddy
```

```
Name: fname, dtype: object
```

```
age over 33:
0    False
1    False
2    False
3    False
4     True
5     True
Name: age, dtype: bool
```

```
age over 33:
   fname  lname  age gender country
4   sara  stein   34      f  france
5   eddy  bower   35      m  france
```

PANDAS DATAFRAMES AND EXCEL SPREADSHEETS

Listing 4.32 displays the content of `people_xslx.py` that illustrates how to read data from an Excel spreadsheet and create a DataFrame with that data.

LISTING 4.32: people_xslx.py

```
import pandas as pd

df = pd.read_excel("people.xlsx")
print("Contents of Excel spreadsheet:")
print(df)
```

Listing 4.32 is straightforward: the DataFrame df is initialized with the contents of the spreadsheet `people.xlsx` (whose contents are the same as `people.csv`) via the Pandas function `read_excel()`. The output from Listing 4.32 is here:

```
   fname  lname  age gender country
0   john  smith   30      m     usa
1   jane  smith   31      f  france
2   jack  jones   32      f  france
3   dave  stone   33      f  france
4   sara  stein   34      f  france
5   eddy  bower   35      f  france
```

SELECT, ADD, AND DELETE COLUMNS IN DATAFRAMES

This section contains short code blocks that illustrate how to perform operations on a DataFrame that resemble the operations in a Python dictionary. For example, getting, setting, and deleting columns works with the same syntax as the analogous Python `dict` operations, as shown here:

```
df = pd.DataFrame.from_dict(dict([('A',[1,2,3]),('B',[4,5,6])]),
```

```
                          orient='index', columns=['one', 'two', 'three'])

print(df)
```

The output from the preceding code snippet is here:

```
     one   two   three
A     1     2       3
B     4     5       6
```

Now look at the following sequence of operations on the contents of the DataFrame df:

```
df['three'] = df['one'] * df['two']
df['flag'] = df['one'] > 2
print(df)
```

The output from the preceding code block is here:

```
     one   two   three    flag
a    1.0   1.0     1.0   False
b    2.0   2.0     4.0   False
c    3.0   3.0     9.0    True
d    NaN   4.0     NaN   False
```

Columns can be deleted or popped like they are with a Python dict, as shown in the following code snippet:

```
del df['two']
three = df.pop('three')
print(df)
```

The output from the preceding code block is here:

```
     one    flag
a    1.0   False
b    2.0   False
c    3.0    True
d    NaN   False
```

When inserting a scalar value, it will naturally be propagated to fill the column:

```
df['foo'] = 'bar'
print(df)
```

The output from the preceding code snippet is here:

```
     one    flag   foo
a    1.0   False   bar
b    2.0   False   bar
c    3.0    True   bar
d    NaN   False   bar
```

When inserting a Series that does not have the same index as the DataFrame, it will be "conformed" to the index of the DataFrame:

```
df['one_trunc'] = df['one'][:2]
print(df)
```

The output from the preceding code snippet is here:

```
   one    flag  foo  one_trunc
a  1.0   False  bar        1.0
b  2.0   False  bar        2.0
c  3.0    True  bar        NaN
d  NaN   False  bar        NaN
```

You can insert raw ndarrays, but their length must match the length of the index of the DataFrame.

PANDAS DATAFRAMES AND SCATTERPLOTS

Listing 4.33 displays the content of pandas_scatter_df.py that illustrates how to generate a scatterplot from a DataFrame.

LISTING 4.33: pandas_scatter_df.py

```
import numpy as np
import pandas as pd
import matplotlib.pyplot as plt
from pandas import read_csv
from pandas.plotting import scatter_matrix

myarray = np.array([[10,30,20], [50,40,60],[1000,2000,3000]])

rownames = ['apples', 'oranges', 'beer']
colnames = ['January', 'February', 'March']

mydf = pd.DataFrame(myarray, index=rownames, columns=colnames)

print(mydf)
print(mydf.describe())

scatter_matrix(mydf)
plt.show()
```

Listing 4.33 starts with various import statements, followed by the definition of the NumPy array myarray. Next, the variables myarray and colnames are initialized with values for the rows and columns, respectively. The next portion of Listing 4.33 initializes the DataFrame mydf so that the rows and columns are labeled in the output, as shown here:

```
January  February  March
apples        10        30      20
oranges       50        40      60
beer        1000      2000    3000
             January     February        March
count       3.000000    3.000000     3.000000
mean      353.333333  690.000000  1026.666667
std       560.386771 1134.504297  1709.073823
min        10.000000   30.000000    20.000000
25%        30.000000   35.000000    40.000000
50%        50.000000   40.000000    60.000000
75%       525.000000 1020.000000  1530.000000
max      1000.000000 2000.000000  3000.0000000
```

PANDAS DATAFRAMES AND SIMPLE STATISTICS

Listing 4.34 displays the content of housing_stats.py that illustrates how to gather basic statistics from data in a DataFrame.

LISTING 4.34: housing_stats.py

```
import pandas as pd

df = pd.read_csv("housing.csv")

minimum_bdrms = df["bedrooms"].min()
median_bdrms  = df["bedrooms"].median()
maximum_bdrms = df["bedrooms"].max()

print("minimum # of bedrooms:",minimum_bdrms)
print("median  # of bedrooms:",median_bdrms)
print("maximum # of bedrooms:",maximum_bdrms)
print("")

print("median values:",df.median().values)
print("")

prices = df["price"]
print("first 5 prices:")
print(prices.head())
print("")

median_price = df["price"].median()
print("median price:",median_price)
print("")

corr_matrix = df.corr()
print("correlation matrix:")
print(corr_matrix["price"].sort_values(ascending=False))
```

Listing 4.34 initializes the DataFrame df with the contents of the CSV file housing.csv. The next three variables are initialized with the minimum, median, and maximum number of bedrooms, respectively, and then these values are displayed.

The next portion of Listing 4.34 initializes the variable `prices` with the contents of the "prices" column of the DataFrame `df`. Next, the first five rows are printed via the `prices.head()` statement, followed by the median value of the prices.

The final portion of Listing 4.34 initializes the variable `corr_matrix` with the contents of the correlation matrix for the DataFrame `df`, and then displays its contents. The output from Listing 4.34 is here:

```
Apples
10
```

USEFUL ONE-LINE COMMANDS IN PANDAS

This section contains an eclectic mix of one-line commands in Pandas (some of which you have already seen in this chapter) that are useful to know.

- Save a DataFrame to a CSV file (comma separated and without indices):
  `df.to_csv("data.csv", sep=",", index=False)`
- List the column names of a DataFrame:
  `df.columns`
- Drop missing data from a DataFrame:
  `df.dropna(axis=0, how='any')`
- Replace missing data in a DataFrame:
  `df.replace(to_replace=None, value=None)`
- Check for NANs in a DataFrame:
  `pd.isnull(object)`
- Drop a feature in a DataFrame:
  `df.drop('feature_variable_name', axis=1)`
- Convert object type to float in a DataFrame:
  `pd.to_numeric(df["feature_name"], errors='coerce')`
- Convert data in a DataFrame to NumPy array:
  `df.as_matrix()`
- Display the first n rows of a DataFrame:
  `df.head(n)`
- Get data by feature name in a DataFrame:
  `df.loc[feature_name]`
- Apply a function to a DataFrame. Multiply all values in the "height" column of the DataFrame by 3:
  `df["height"].apply(lambda height: 3 * height)`

  OR:

  ```
  def multiply(x):
  return x * 3
  df["height"].apply(multiply)
  ```
- Rename the fourth column of the DataFrame as "height:"
  `df.rename(columns = {df.columns[3]:'height'},`
  `inplace=True)`

- Get the unique entries of the column "first" in a DataFrame:
  ```
  df[""first"].unique()
  ```
- Create a DataFrame with columns "first" and "last" from an existing DataFrame:
  ```
  new_df = df[["name", "size"]]
  ```
- Sort the data in a DataFrame:
  ```
  df.sort_values(ascending = False)
  ```
- Filter the data column named "size" to display only values equal to 7:
  ```
  df[df["size"] == 7]
  ```
- Select the first row of the "height" column in a DataFrame:
  ```
  df.loc([0], ['height'])
  ```

WORKING WITH BARD

This section provides a preview of several Bard-generated Python code samples. As you saw in Chapter 3, more comprehensive descriptions of generative AI, Gemini, and Bard are available in Chapter 5. In addition, Chapter 6 is devoted to Bard-generated Python code samples.

The three Python code samples that you will see in the subsequent sections are listed below:

- Pandas DataFrame with Random Values
- Pandas DataFrame and a Bar Chart
- Pandas DataFrame and Statistics

A Pandas DataFrame with Random Values

The code sample that Bard generated in this section is based on the following prompt for Bard:

```
Please generate Python code that counts the number of
digits, upper case letters, and lower case Letters in a
randomly generated string, and provide an explanation of
the Python code.
```

Listing 4.35 shows the content of bard_random_df.py that displays the sum of the rows and columns in a DataFrame that contains randomly generated numbers.

Keep in mind that the contents of Listing 4.35 (and subsequent samples in this chapter and Chapter 6) are presented "as-is:" the content and layout are what you will see in Bard.

LISTING 4.35: bard_random_df.py

```
import pandas as pd
import numpy as np

# Define number of rows and columns
nrows = 4
ncols = 5
```

```python
# Generate random data
np.random.seed(1)
data = np.random.randint(1, 100, size=(nrows, ncols))

# Create Pandas DataFrame
df = pd.DataFrame(data)

# Calculate row sums
row_sums = df.sum(axis=1)

# Calculate column sums
column_sums = df.sum(axis=0)

# Add row and column sums to the DataFrame
df['Row Sum'] = row_sums
df.loc['Column Sum'] = column_sums

# Print the DataFrame with row and column sums
print("DataFrame with row and column sums:")
print(df)
"""
```

Explanation:
    Import libraries:
        We import pandas for data manipulation and numpy
    for generating random numbers.
        Define parameters:
            We set the number of rows (nrows) and columns
    (ncols) for the DataFrame.
        Generate random data:
            We use np.random.seed(1) to ensure reproducibility
    of the random numbers.
            Then, we use np.random.randint(1, 100, size=(nrows,
    ncols)) to generate an array of random integers between 1
    and 100 with the specified number of rows and columns.
        Create Pandas DataFrame:
            We use pd.DataFrame(data) to convert the generated
    NumPy array into a Pandas DataFrame.
        Calculate row and column sums:
            We use df.sum(axis=1) to calculate the sum of each
    row and store the results in a Series object named row_sums.
            We use df.sum(axis=0) to calculate the sum of each
    column and store the results in another Series object named
    column_sums.
        Add row and column sums to the DataFrame:
            We add a new column named 'Row Sum' to the
    DataFrame and populate it with the values in row_sums.
            We use df.loc['Column Sum'] = column_sums to add a
    new row named 'Column Sum' to the DataFrame and populate it
    with the values in column_sums.
        Print the DataFrame:
            We use print(df) to display the DataFrame with the
    row and column sums included.

This code generates a Pandas DataFrame with randomly
generated numbers and calculates the sum of each row and
column. You can modify this code to suit your specific
needs, such as changing the range of random numbers, adding
more calculations, or customizing the DataFrame formatting.

Bard may display inaccurate info, including about people,
so double-check its responses.

"""

Launch the code in Listing 4.35, and you will see output that is similar to the following output (which depends on the specific string):

```
DataFrame with row and column sums:
                 0       1       2       3       4    Row Sum
0             38.0    13.0    73.0    10.0    76.0      210.0
1              6.0    80.0    65.0    17.0     2.0      170.0
2             77.0    72.0     7.0    26.0    51.0      233.0
3             21.0    19.0    85.0    12.0    29.0      166.0
Column Sum   142.0   184.0   230.0    65.0   158.0        NaN
```

Pandas DataFrame and a Bar Chart

The code sample that Bard generated in this section is based on the following prompt:

Please generate Python code that creates a Pandas dataframe with 4 rows and 5 columns of randomly generated numbers and then calculates the sum of each row and the sum of each column, as well as a bar chart with the data in the dataframe, along with an explanation of the Python code.

Listing 4.36 shows the content of bard_random_df_barchart.py, which displays the sum of the rows and columns in a DataFrame that contains randomly generated numbers.

LISTING 4.36: bard_random_df_barchart.py

```python
import pandas as pd
import numpy as np
import matplotlib.pyplot as plt

# Define number of rows and columns
nrows = 4
ncols = 5

# Generate random data
np.random.seed(1)
data = np.random.randint(1, 100, size=(nrows, ncols))

# Create Pandas DataFrame
df = pd.DataFrame(data)

# Calculate row and column sums
row_sums = df.sum(axis=1)
column_sums = df.sum(axis=0)

# Add row and column sums to the DataFrame
df['Row Sum'] = row_sums
df.loc['Column Sum'] = column_sums

# Create a bar chart

  plt.figure(figsize=(10, 6))
```

```
df.plot(kind='bar', stacked=False)
plt.title("Bar Chart of Random Data")
plt.xlabel("Columns")
plt.ylabel("Values")
plt.xticks(rotation=0)
plt.tight_layout()

# Print the DataFrame
print("DataFrame with row and column sums:")
print(df)

# Show the bar chart
plt.show()

"""
```

Explanation:
    Imports:
        pandas is imported to work with DataFrames.
        numpy is imported to generate random numbers.
        matplotlib.pyplot is imported to create the bar chart.

    Define parameters:
        nrows and ncols define the number of rows and columns in the DataFrame.

    Generate random data:
        np.random.seed(1) ensures reproducibility of the random numbers.
        np.random.randint(1, 100, size=(nrows, ncols)) generates a NumPy array with random integers between 1 and 100, with nrows rows and ncols columns.

    Create Pandas DataFrame:
        pd.DataFrame(data) converts the NumPy array to a Pandas DataFrame.

    Calculate row and column sums:
        df.sum(axis=1) calculates the sum of each row and stores them in a Series object named row_sums.
        df.sum(axis=0) calculates the sum of each column and stores them in a Series object named column_sums.

    Add sums to DataFrame:
        A new column 'Row Sum' is added to the DataFrame with the row_sums values.
        A new row named 'Column Sum' is added to the DataFrame with the column_sums values, using the loc method.

    Create a bar chart:
        plt.figure(figsize=(10, 6)) sets the figure size for the plot.

```
        df.plot(kind='bar', stacked=False) creates a bar
chart using the values in the DataFrame.
        plt.title("Bar Chart of Random Data") sets the
title of the chart.
        plt.xlabel("Columns") and plt.ylabel("Values") set
the labels for the x and y axes.
        plt.xticks(rotation=0) ensures all column labels
are visible.
        plt.tight_layout() adjusts the layout to avoid
overlapping elements.

    Print the DataFrame and show the bar chart:
        The DataFrame with row and column sums is printed.
        plt.show() displays the bar chart.
"""
```

Now launch the code in Listing 4.36, and you will see output that is similar to the following output (which depends on the randomly generated values):

```
DataFrame with row and column sums:
                 0       1       2       3       4    Row Sum
0             38.0    13.0    73.0    10.0    76.0     210.0
1              6.0    80.0    65.0    17.0     2.0     170.0
2             77.0    72.0     7.0    26.0    51.0     233.0
3             21.0    19.0    85.0    12.0    29.0     166.0
Column Sum   142.0   184.0   230.0    65.0   158.0       NaN
```

In addition to the preceding output, you will see the bar chart that is displayed in Figure 4.1.

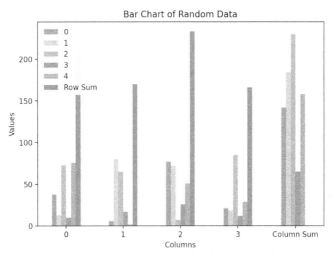

FIGURE 4.1: A bar chart rendered via Matplotlib

Pandas DataFrames and Statistics

The code sample that Bard generated in this section is based on the following prompt:

Please generate Python code that creates a Pandas dataframe with 4 rows and 5 columns of randomly generated numbers and then calculates the mean, variance, and standard deviation of the numbers in each column of the dataframe, along with an explanation of the Python code.

Listing 4.37 displays the content of `bard_random_statistics.py` that shows the sum of the rows and columns in a DataFrame that contains randomly generated numbers.

LISTING 4.37: bard_random_statistics.py

```python
import pandas as pd
import numpy as np

# Define number of rows and columns
nrows = 4
ncols = 5

# Generate random data
np.random.seed(1)
data = np.random.randint(1, 100, size=(nrows, ncols))

# Create Pandas DataFrame
df = pd.DataFrame(data)

# Calculate descriptive statistics for each column
for col in df.columns:
    # Calculate mean, variance, and standard deviation
    mean = df[col].mean()
    variance = df[col].var()
    std_dev = df[col].std()

    # Print the results
    print(f"Column {col}:")
    print(f"\tMean: {mean:.2f}")
    print(f"\tVariance: {variance:.2f}")
    print(f"\tStandard Deviation: {std_dev:.2f}")
    print("")

"""
Explanation:
    Import libraries:
        We import pandas for data manipulation and numpy
for generating random numbers.
    Define parameters:
        We set the number of rows (nrows) and columns
(ncols) for the DataFrame.
    Generate random data:
        We use np.random.seed(1) to ensure reproducibility
of the random numbers.
```

Then, we use np.random.randint(1, 100, size=(nrows, ncols)) to generate an array of random integers between 1 and 100 with the specified number of rows and columns.
  Create Pandas DataFrame:
    We use pd.DataFrame(data) to convert the generated NumPy array into a Pandas DataFrame.
  Calculate descriptive statistics for each column:
    We iterate through each column of the DataFrame using a for loop.
    For each column, we calculate the following descriptive statistics:
        mean: using df[col].mean()
        variance: using df[col].var()
        standard deviation: using df[col].std()
    We format the results to two decimal places and print them.

This code will generate a Pandas DataFrame with randomly generated numbers and then calculate the mean, variance, and standard deviation for each column. You can modify this code to calculate other descriptive statistics or to perform different operations on the DataFrame.

Bard may display inaccurate info, including about people, so double-check its responses.
"""

Now launch the code in Listing 4.37, and you will see output that is similar to the following output (which depends on the randomly generated values):

```
Column 0:
        Mean: 35.50
        Variance: 936.33
        Standard Deviation: 30.60

Column 1:
        Mean: 46.00
        Variance: 1216.67
        Standard Deviation: 34.88

Column 2:
        Mean: 57.50
        Variance: 1201.00
        Standard Deviation: 34.66

Column 3:
        Mean: 16.25
        Variance: 50.92
        Standard Deviation: 7.14
```

```
Column 4:
        Mean: 39.50
        Variance: 993.67
        Standard Deviation: 31.52
```

SUMMARY

This chapter introduced you to Pandas for creating labeled DataFrames and displaying the metadata of DataFrames. Then you learned how to create DataFrames from various sources of data, such as random numbers and hard-coded data values.

You also learned how to read Excel spreadsheets and perform numeric calculations on that data, such as the minimum, mean, and maximum values in numeric columns. You saw how to create DataFrames from data stored in CSV files. Then you learned how to invoke a Web service to retrieve data and populate a DataFrame with that data. In addition, you learned how to generate a scatterplot from data in a DataFrame.

## CHAPTER 5

GENERATIVE AI, BARD, AND GEMINI

This chapter contains information (some of which is AI-generated) about the main features of Bard, as well as some of its competitors.

The first portion of this chapter starts with information (generated by Bard) regarding the nature of generative AI and conversational AI versus generative AI. According to Bard, it is true that Bard itself is included in generative AI.

The second portion of this chapter provides an overview of Gemini, followed by an introduction to Bard and some of its features, as well as some alternatives to Bard.

WHAT IS GENERATIVE AI?

Generative AI refers to a subset of artificial intelligence models and techniques that are designed to generate new data samples that are similar in nature to a given set of input data. The goal is to produce content or data that was not part of the original training set, but is coherent, contextually relevant, and in the same style or structure.

Generative AI is arguably unique in its ability to create and innovate with information, as opposed to merely analyzing or classifying it. The advancements in this field have led to breakthroughs in creative domains and practical applications, making it a cutting-edge area of AI research and development.

Key Features of Generative AI

The following list contains key features of generative AI, followed by a brief description for each item:

- Data generation
- Synthesis
- Learning distributions

Data generation refers to the ability to create new data points that are not part of the training data but resemble it. This can include text, images, music, videos, or any other form of data.

Synthesis means that generative models can blend various inputs to generate outputs that incorporate features from each input, like merging the styles of two images.

Learning distributions means that generative AI models learn the probability distribution of the training data so they can produce new samples from that distribution.

Popular Techniques in Generative AI

Generative Adversarial Networks (GANs): GANs consist of two networks, a generator and a discriminator, that are trained simultaneously. The generator tries to produce fake data, while the discriminator tries to distinguish between real data and fake data. Over time, the generator gets better at producing realistic data.

Variational Autoencoders (VAEs): VAEs are probabilistic models that learn to encode and decode data in a manner so that the encoded representations can be used to generate new data samples.

Recurrent Neural Networks (RNNs): Used primarily for sequence generation, such as text or music.

What Makes Generative AI Unique

Creation vs. Classification: While most traditional AI models aim to classify input data into predefined categories, generative models aim to create new data.

Unsupervised Learning: Many generative models, especially GANs and VAEs, operate in an unsupervised manner, meaning they do not require labeled data for training.

Diverse Outputs: Generative models can produce a wide variety of outputs based on learned distributions, making them ideal for tasks like art generation, style transfer, and more.

Challenges: Generative AI poses unique challenges, such as mode collapse in GANs or ensuring the coherence of generated content.

Furthermore, there are numerous areas that involve generative AI applications, some of which are listed in the following list:

• Art and music creation
• Data augmentation
• Style transfer
• Text generation
• Image synthesis
• Drug discovery

Art and music creation includes generating paintings, music, or other forms of art.

Data augmentation involves creating additional data for training models, especially when the original dataset is limited.

Style transfer refers to applying the style of one image to the content of another.

Text generation is a popular application of generative AI that involves creating coherent and contextually relevant text.

Image synthesis is another popular area of generative AI, and it involves generating realistic images, faces, or even creating scenes for video games.

Drug discovery is an important facet of generative AI that pertains to generating molecular structures for new potential drugs.

CONVERSATIONAL AI VERSUS GENERATIVE AI

Both conversational AI and generative AI are prominent subfields within the broader domain of artificial intelligence. However, these subfields have a different focus regarding their primary objective, the technologies that they use, and applications. Please read the following article for more information:

https://medium.com/@social_65128/differences-between-conversational-ai-and-generative-ai-e3adca2a8e9a

The primary differences between the two subfields are in the following sequence of points:

- Primary objective
- Applications
- Technologies used
- Training and Interaction
- Evaluation
- Data requirements

Primary Objective

The main goal of conversational AI is to facilitate human-like interactions between machines and humans. This includes chatbots, virtual assistants, and other systems that engage in dialogues with users.

The primary objective of generative AI is to create new content or data that was not in the training set but is not necessarily similar in structure and style to the original data. This can range from generating images, music, and text to more complex tasks like video synthesis.

Applications

Common applications for conversational AI include customer support chatbots, voice-operated virtual assistants (like Siri or Alexa), and interactive voice response (IVR) systems.

There is a broad spectrum of common applications for generative AI, such as creating art or music, generating realistic video game environments, synthesizing voices, and producing realistic images or even deep fakes.

Technologies Used

Conversational AI often relies on Natural Language Processing (NLP) techniques to understand and generate human language. This includes intent recognition, entity extraction, and dialogue management.

Generative AI commonly utilizes Generative Adversarial Networks (GANs), Variational Autoencoders (VAEs), and other generative models to produce new content.

Training and Interaction

While training can be supervised, semi-supervised, or unsupervised, the primary interaction mode for conversational AI is through back-and-forth dialogue or conversation.

The training process for generative AI, especially with models like GANs, involves iterative processes where the model learns to generate data by trying to fool a discriminator into believing the generated data is real.

Evaluation

Conversational AI evaluation metrics often revolve around understanding and response accuracy, user satisfaction, and the fluency of generated responses.

Generative AI evaluation metrics for models like GANs can be challenging and might involve using a combination of quantitative metrics and human judgment to assess the quality of generated content.

Data Requirements

Data requirements for conversational AI typically involve dialogue data from conversations between humans or between humans and bots.

Data requirements for generative AI involve large datasets of the kind of content it is supposed to generate, such as images, text, or music.

Although both conversational AI and generative AI deal with generating outputs, their primary objectives, applications, and methodologies can differ significantly. Conversational AI is used for interactive communication with users, while generative AI focuses on producing new, original content.

IS GEMINI PART OF GENERATIVE AI?

Gemini is an LLM that is considered an example of generative AI. Bard belongs to a class of models called "transformers," which are particularly adept at handling sequences of data, such as text-related tasks.

The following list provides various reasons why Gemini is considered generative, followed by a brief description of each item:

- Text generation
- Learning distributions
- Broad applications
- Unsupervised learning

Text Generation: These models can produce coherent, contextually relevant, and often highly sophisticated sequences of text based on given prompts. They generate responses that were not explicitly present in their training data but are constructed based on the patterns and structures they learned during training.

Learning Distributions: Gemini (as well as GPT-3, GPT-4, and similar models) learn the probability distribution of their training data. When generating text, they are essentially sampling from this learned distribution to produce sequences that are likely based on their training.

Broad Applications: Beyond just text-based chat or conversation, these models can be used for a variety of generative tasks like story writing, code generation, poetry, and even creating content in specific styles or mimicking certain authors, showcasing their generative capabilities.

Unsupervised Learning: While they can be fine-tuned with specific datasets, models like GPT-3 are primarily trained in an unsupervised manner on vast amounts of text, learning to generate content without requiring explicit labeled data for every possible response.

In essence, Google Gemini is a quintessential example of generative AI in the realm of NLP and generation.

The next several sections briefly introduce some of the AI companies that have a strong presence in the market.

DEEPMIND

DeepMind has made significant contributions to AI, which includes the creation of various AI systems. DeepMind was established in 2010 and became a subsidiary of Google 2014, and its home page is at *https://deepmind.com/*.

DeepMind created the 280 GB language model Gopher, which significantly outperformed its competitors, including GPT-3, J1-Jumbo, and MT-NLG. DeepMind also developed AlphaFold, which solved a protein folding task that had eluded researchers for ten years in only 30 minutes. Moreover, DeepMind made AlphaFold available for free for everyone in July 2021. DeepMind has made significant contributions in the development of AI game systems, some of which are discussed in the next section.

DeepMind and Games

DeepMind powers the AI systems AlphaStar, which plays StarCraft, and AlphaGo, which defeated the best human players in Go (the game is considerably more difficult than chess). These games provide "perfect information," whereas games with "imperfect information" (such as poker) have posed challenges for ML models.

AlphaGo Zero (the successor of AlphaGo) mastered the game through self-play in less time and with less computing power than AlphaGo. AlphaGo Zero exhibited extraordinary performance by defeating AlphaGo 100 - 0. Another powerful system is AlphaZero, which used a self-play technique to learn to play Go, chess, and shogi, and also achieved SOTA (State Of The Art) performance results.

By way of comparison, ML models that use tree search are well-suited for games with perfect information. Games with imperfect information (such as poker) involve hidden information that can be leveraged to devise counter strategies to counteract the strategies of opponents. In particular, AlphaStar is capable of playing against the best players of StarCraft II, and became the first AI to achieve SOTA results in a game that requires a highly strategic methodology.

Player of Games (PoG)

The DeepMind team at Google devised the general-purpose PoG (Player of Games) algorithm that is based on the following techniques:

- CFR (counterfactual regret minimization)
- CVPN (counterfactual value-and-policy network)
- GT-CFT (growing tree CFR)
- CVPN

The counterfactual value-and-policy network (CVPN) is a neural network that calculates the counterfactuals for each state belief in the game. This is important for evaluating the different variants of the game at any given time.

Growing tree CFR (GT-CFR) is a variation of CFR that is optimized for game-trees trees that grow over time. GT-CFR is based on two fundamental phases, which is discussed in more detail online:

https://medium.com/syncedreview/deepminds-pog-excels-in-perfect-and-imperfect-information-games-advancing-research-on-general-9dbad5c04221

OPENAI

OpenAI is an AI research company that has made significant contributions to AI, including DALL-E and Bard, and its home page is at *https://openai.com/api/*.

OpenAI was founded in San Francisco by Elon Musk and Sam Altman (as well as others), and one of its stated goals is to develop AI that benefits humanity. Given Microsoft's massive investments in and deep alliance with the organization, OpenAI might be viewed as an arm of Microsoft. OpenAI is the creator of the GPT-x series of LLMs (Large Language Models), as well as Bard, which was made available on November 30, 2022.

In addition, OpenAI developed DALL-E, which generates images from text. OpenAI initially did not permit users to upload images that contained realistic faces. Later (in the fourth quarter of 2022), OpenAI changed its policy to allow users to upload faces into its online system. Check the OpenAI Web page for more details.

OpenAI has also released a public beta of Embeddings, which is a data format that is suitable for various types of tasks with machine learning, as described here:

https://beta.openai.com/docs/guides/embeddings

OpenAI is the creator of Codex, which provides a set of models that were trained using NLP. The initial release of Codex was in private beta, and more information is accessible at *https://beta.openai.com/docs/engines/ instruct-series-beta*.

OpenAI offers four models that are collectively called their "Instruct" models, which support the ability of GPT-3 to generate natural language. These models will be deprecated in early January 2024 and replaced with updated versions of GPT-3, Bard, and GPT-4.

If you want to learn more about the features and services that OpenAI offers, navigate to the following website: *https://platform.openai.com/ overview*.

COHERE

Cohere is a start-up and a competitor of OpenAI, and its home page is at *https://cohere.ai/*.

Cohere develops cutting-edge NLP technology that is commercially available for multiple industries. Cohere is focused on models that perform textual analysis instead of models for text generation (such as GPT-based models). The founding team of Cohere is impressive: CEO Aidan Gomez is one of the co-inventors of the transformer architecture, and CTO Nick Frost is a protege of Geoff Hinton.

HUGGING FACE

Hugging Face is a popular community-based repository for open-source NLP technology, and its home page is at *https://github.com/huggingface*.

Unlike OpenAI or Cohere, Hugging Face does not build its own NLP models. Instead, Hugging Face is a platform that manages a plethora of open-source NLP models that customers can fine-tune and then deploy those fine-tuned models. Indeed, Hugging Face has become the eminent location for people to collaborate on NLP models because of the plethora of LLMs that it makes available to users.

Hugging Face Libraries

Hugging Face offers three important libraries: datasets, tokenizers, and transformers. The Accelerate library supports PyTorch models. The datasets library provides an assortment of libraries for NLP. The tokenizers library enables you to convert text data to numeric values.

Perhaps the most impressive library is the transformers library, which provides an enormous set of pre-trained BERT-based models that can perform a wide variety of NLP tasks. The Github repository is available at *https://github.com/huggingface/transformers*.

Hugging Face Model Hub

Hugging Face provides a model hub that offers a plethora of models that are accessible online. Moreover, the website supports online testing of its models, which includes the following tasks:

- Masked word completion with BERT
- Name Entity Recognition with Electra
- Natural Language Inference with RoBERTa
- Question answering with DistilBERT
- Summarization with BART
- Text generation with GPT-2
- Translation with T5

Navigate to the following website and follow the guidelines in order to see the text generation capabilities of "writing with a transformer:" *https://transformer.huggingface.co*.

In a subsequent chapter, you will see Python code samples that show how to list all the available Hugging Face datasets as well as how to load a specific dataset.

AI21

AI21 is a company that provides proprietary large language models via API to support the applications of its customers. The current SOTA model of AI21 is called Jurassic-1 (roughly the same size as GPT-3), and AI21 also creates its own applications on top of Jurassic-1 and other models. The current application suite of AI21 involves tools that can augment reading and writing.

Primer is an older competitor in this space, founded two years before the invention of the transformer. The company primarily serves clients in government and defense.

INFLECTIONAI

A newer AI company is InflectionAI, whose highly impressive founding team includes

- Reid Hoffman (LinkedIn)
- DeepMind cofounder Mustafa Suleyman
- DeepMind researcher Karen Simonyan

InflectionAI is committed to a challenging task: enabling humans to interact with computers in much the same way that humans communicate with each other.

ANTHROPIC

Anthropic was created in 2021 by former employees of OpenAI, and its home page is at *https://www.anthropic.com/*.

Anthropic has significant financial support from an assortment of companies, including Google and Salesforce. As this book goes to print, Anthropic released Claude 2 as a competitor to Bard.

Claude 2 has the ability to summarize as much as 75,000 words of text-based content, whereas Bard currently has a limit of 3,000 words. Moreover, Claude 2 achieved a score of 76.5% on portions of the bar exam and 71% in a Python coding test. Claude 2 also has a higher rate than Bard in terms of providing "clean" responses to queries from users.

This concludes the portion of the chapter regarding the AI companies that are making important contributions in AI. The next section provides a high-level introduction to LLMs (large language models).

WHAT IS PROMPT ENGINEERING?

We have already discussed text generators such as GPT-3 and DALL-E 2 from OpenAI, Jurassic from AI21, and Midjourney and Stable Diffusion, which can perform text-to-image generation. *Prompt engineering* refers to devising text-based prompts that enable AI-based systems to improve the output that is generated, which means that the output more closely matches whatever users want to produce from AI-systems. By way of analogy, think of prompts as similar to the role of coaches: they offer advice and suggestions to help people perform better in their given tasks.

Since prompts are based on words, the challenge involves learning how different words can affect the generated output. Moreover, it is difficult to predict how systems respond to a given prompt. For instance, if you want to generate a landscape, the difference between a dark landscape and a bright landscape is intuitive. However, if you want a beautiful landscape, how would an AI system generate a corresponding image? As you can surmise, concrete words are easier than abstract or subjective words for AI systems that generate images from text. Just to add more detail to the previous example, how would you visualize the following images?

- A beautiful landscape
- A beautiful song
- A beautiful movie

Although prompt engineering started with text-to-image generation, there are other types of prompt engineering, such as audio-based prompts, that interpret emphasized text and emotions that are detected in speech, and sketch-based prompts that generate images from drawings. The most recent focus of attention involves text-based prompts for generating videos, which presents exciting opportunities for artists and designers. An example of image-to-image processing is accessible online at the following site:

https://huggingface.co/spaces/fffiloni/stable-diffusion-color-sketch

Prompts and Completions

A *prompt* is a text string that users provide to LLMs, and a *completion* is the text that users receive from LLMs. Prompts assist LLMs in completing a request (task), and they can vary in length. Although prompts can be any text string, including a random string, the quality and structure of prompts affects the quality of completions.

Think of prompts as a mechanism for giving "guidance" to LLMs or even as a way to "coach" LLMs into providing desired answers. Keep in mind that the number of tokens in a prompt plus the number of tokens in the completion can be at most 2,048 tokens.

Types of Prompts

The following list contains well-known types prompts for LLMs:

- zero-shot prompts
- one-shot prompts
- few-shot prompts
- instruction prompts

A *zero-shot prompt* contains a description of a task, whereas a *one-shot prompt* consists of a single example for completing a task. As you can probably surmise, *few-shot prompts* consist of multiple examples (typically between 10 and 100). In all cases, a clear description of the task or tasks is recommended: more tasks provide GPT-3 with more information, which in turn can lead to more accurate completions.

T0 (for "zero shot") is an interesting LLM: although T0 is 16 times smaller (11 GB) than GPT-3 (175 GB), T0 has outperformed GPT-3 on language-related tasks. T0 can perform well on unseen NLP tasks (i.e., tasks that are new to T0) because it was trained on a dataset containing multiple tasks.

The following set of links provide the Github repository for T0, a Web page for training T0 directly in a browser, and a 3 GB version of T0, respectively:

https://github.com/bigscience-workshop/t-zero

As you can probably surmise, T0++ is based on T0, and it was trained with extra tasks beyond the set of tasks on which T0 was trained.

Here is another detail to keep in mind: the first three prompts in the preceding list are also called *zero-shot learning*, *one-shot learning*, and *few-shot learning*.

Instruction Prompts

Instruction prompts are used for fine tuning LLMs, and they specify a format (determined by you) for the manner in which the LLM is expected to conform in its responses. You can prepare your own instruction prompts or you can access prompt template libraries that contain different templates for different tasks, along with different data sets. Various prompt instruction templates are publicly available, such as the following links that provides prompt templates for Llama:

https://github.com/devbrones/llama-prompts

https://pub.towardsai.net/llama-gpt4all-simplified-local-Bard-ab7d28d34923

Reverse Prompts

Another technique uses a reverse order: input prompts are answers, and the responses are the questions associated with the answers (similar to a popular game show). For example, given a French sentence, you might ask the model, "What English text might have resulted in this French translation?"

System Prompts Versus Agent Prompts

The distinction between a system prompt and an agent prompt often comes up in the context of conversational AI systems and chatbot design.

A *system prompt* is typically an initial message or cue given by the system to guide the user on what they can do or to set expectations about the interaction. It often serves as an introduction or a way to guide users on how to proceed. Here are some examples of system prompts:

- "Welcome to ChatBotX! You can ask me questions about weather, news, or sports. How can I assist you today?"
- "Hello! For account details, press 1. For technical support, press 2."
- "Greetings! Type 'order' to track your package or 'help' for assistance."

By contrast, an *agent prompt* is a message generated by the AI model or agent in response to a user's input during the course of an interaction. It is a part of the back-and-forth exchange within the conversation. The agent prompt guides the user to provide more information, clarifies ambiguity, or nudges the user towards a specific action. Here are some examples of agent prompts:

- User: "I'm looking for shoes."
  Agent Prompt: "Great! Are you looking for men's or women's shoes?"
- User: "I can't log in."
  Agent Prompt: "I'm sorry to hear that. Can you specify if you're having trouble with your password or username?"
- User: "Tell me a joke."
  Agent Prompt: "Why did the chicken join a band? Because it had the drumsticks!"

The fundamental difference between the two is their purpose and place-ment in the interaction. A system prompt is often at the beginning of an interaction, setting the stage for the conversation. An agent prompt occurs during the conversation, steering the direction of the dialogue based on user input.

Both types of prompts are crucial for creating a fluid and intuitive conver-sational experience for users. They guide the user and help ensure that the system understands and addresses the user's needs effectively.

Prompt Templates

Prompt templates are predefined formats or structures used to instruct a model or system to perform a specific task. They serve as a foundation for generating prompts, where certain parts of the template can be filled in or customized to produce a variety of specific prompts. By way of analogy, prompt templates are the counterpart to macros that you can define in some text editors.

Prompt templates are especially useful when working with language mod-els, as they provide a consistent way to query the model across multiple tasks or data points. In particular, prompt templates can make it easier to

- ensure consistency when querying a model multiple times
- facilitate batch processing or automation
- reduce errors and variations in how questions are posed to the model

As an example, suppose you're working with an LLM and you want to translate English sentences into French. An associated prompt template could be the following:

"Translate the following English sentence into French: {sentence}"

Note that {sentence} is a placeholder that you can replace with any English sentence.

You can use the preceding prompt template to generate specific prompts:

- "Translate the following English sentence into French: 'Hello, how are you?'"
- "Translate the following English sentence into French: 'I love ice cream.'"

As you can see, prompt templates enable you to easily generate a variety of prompts for different sentences without having to rewrite the entire instruc-tion each time. In fact, this concept can be extended to more complex tasks and can incorporate multiple placeholders or more intricate structures, depending on the application.

Poorly-Worded Prompts

When crafting prompts, it is crucial to be as clear and specific as possible to guide the response in the desired direction. Ambiguous or vague prompts can lead to a wide range of responses, many of which might not be useful or relevant to the user's actual intent.

Moreover, poorly-worded prompts are often vague, ambiguous, or too broad, and they can lead to confusion, misunderstanding, or non-specific responses from AI models. Here is a list of examples of poorly-worded prompts:

"Tell me about that thing."
Problem: Too vague. What "thing" is being referred to?

"Why did it happen?"
Problem: No context. What event or situation is being discussed?

"Explain stuff."
Problem: Too broad. What specific "stuff" should be explained?

"Do what is needful."
Problem: Ambiguous. What specific action is required?

"I want information."
Problem: Not specific. What type of information is desired?

"Can you get me the thing from the place?"
Problem: Both "thing" and "place" are unclear.

"Can you tell me about 'What's-his-name's' book?"
Problem: Ambiguous reference. Who is "his?"

"How do you do the process?"
Problem: Which "process" is being referred to?

"Describe the importance of the topic."
Problem: The "topic" is not specified.

"Why is it bad or good?"
Problem: No context. What is "it"?

"Help with the issue."
Problem: Vague. What specific issue is being faced?

"Things to consider for the task."
Problem: Ambiguous. What "task" is being discussed?

"How does this work?"
Problem: Lack of specificity. What is "this?"

WHAT IS GEMINI?

Gemini is the most advanced LLM from Google and is the foundation for Bard. Google plans to integrate Gemini into some of its other products, such as YouTube and Google Search.

Gemini is available in three sizes: *Nano* for mobile devices (such as Pixel 8), *Pro* for Bard, and *Ultra*, the most sophisticated of the three models (which will be available next year).

Gemini is a multimodal LLM that can process various types of input, including text, code, audio, images, and videos. Gemini generated some of the Python code samples in Chapters 3 and 4, as well as all the Python code samples in Chapter 6. However, some of the multimodal features of Gemini will become available at a later point in time. Gemini also sometimes suffers from so-called "hallucinations," which is common for LLMs.

Gemini Ultra Versus GPT-4

Google performed a comparison of Gemini Ultra and GPT-4 from OpenAI, and Ultra outperformed GPT-4 on seven of eight text-based tests. Moreover, Ultra outperformed GPT-4 on ten out of ten multimodal tests. In many cases, Ultra outperformed GPT-4 by a fairly small margin, which means that both LLMs are competitive in terms of functionality. Note that thus far Google has not provided a comparison of Gemini Pro or Gemini Nano with GPT-4.

Gemini Strengths

As you probably expected, Gemini has strengths and weaknesses, just like any other LLM. This section provides a brief description of the major strengths of Gemini.

1. *Accuracy and factuality*: Bard was trained on a massive dataset of text and code, including factual information from Google Search. This allows it to provide accurate and reliable answers to factual questions.

2. *Comprehensiveness*: Bard provides more comprehensive and detailed answers than other large language models. It retrieves relevant information from its database and presents it in a clear and concise manner.

3. *User-friendly interface*: Bard has a user-friendly interface that is easy to navigate and use. It allows users to edit their questions, upvote and downvote responses, and search for information on the Web.

4. *Multiple response formats*: Bard can generate text in various formats, including poems, code, scripts, musical pieces, emails, and letters. This makes it versatile and adaptable to different tasks.

5. *Free to use*: Bard is currently free to use, which makes it accessible to a wide audience.

Gemini's Weaknesses

The previous section discusses the strengths of Gemini, whereas this section provides a brief description of the major weaknesses of Gemini.

1. *Creativity*: While Bard can generate creative text formats, it sometimes lacks originality and can be repetitive. It struggles with tasks that require a high level of imagination and out-of-the-box thinking.

2. *Conversational flow*: Bard can be unnatural in conversations. Its responses may not always flow smoothly or follow the context of the conversation.

3. *Technical knowledge*: Although trained on a massive dataset, Bard can struggle with technical questions or tasks that require specialized knowledge in specific domains.

4. *Limited integrations*: Compared to ChatGPT, Bard has fewer integrations with other apps and services. This limits its functionality and flexibility.

5. *Limited customizability*: Users currently have limited options to customize Bard's behavior or preferences.

Gemini Nano on Mobile Devices

Gemini Nano has features such as grammar correction, proofreading, and text summarization. Moreover, a software update for the Android Pixel 8 Pro is available to provide access to Gemini Nano on mobile devices. Other features will be supported on mobile devices in the coming months.

Google has also created Android AICore, which is a system service that provides access to Nano on Android devices. This service supports improved safety and model management in a manner that makes it easier for you to incorporate AI into Android devices.

WHAT IS BARD?

Bard has been updated with Gemini Pro, which is one of the three Gemini LLMs that are available from Google. Navigate to the following URL to access Bard:

https://bard.google.com/chat/2d66dfbbf91ab734

Currently, Bard is not multimodal: it only supports text prompts. Moreover, Bard is only available in English, which will be expanded at a later date.

Gemini Pro is now available for cloud-based services, such as Google AI Studio as well as Google Cloud Vertex AI: navigate to their respective home pages for additional details. Google says it aims to add Gemini Ultra to Bard in 2024. It will be able to handle different modal types, from images to audio, and will "think more carefully before answering" tricky questions. This version will be called Bard Advanced.

Gemini Pro in Google Bard is free and does not require any payment or credit system to use. Likewise, the Gemini Nano came to the Pixel 8 Pro smartphone in a free update.

It is possible that Google will charge for Gemini Ultra given its more powerful capabilities, in a similar way to how OpenAI charges $20 a month for access to ChatGPT Plus. Thus far, there has been no official statement about this from Google: periodically check online for any updates from Google.

In terms of functionality, Bard can perform a multitude of tasks, some of which are listed below:

- write poetry
- write essays
- write code
- role play
- reject inappropriate requests

Bard also provides "prompt replies," which are examples of what you can ask Bard.

SAMPLE QUERIES AND RESPONSES FROM BARD

The following section has five examples of various queries submitted to Bard, followed by the detailed response from Bard.

EXAMPLE 1

User: Many people think that AI is dangerous. What do you think?
Bard: Whether AI is dangerous is a complex question with no easy answer. There are valid arguments on both sides of the debate.

Potential dangers of AI:

- **Job displacement:** As AI becomes more sophisticated, it has the potential to automate many tasks currently performed by humans, leading to widespread job losses. This could have significant social and economic consequences.
- **Bias and discrimination:** AI systems can inherit and amplify biases present in the data they are trained on. This could lead to discriminatory outcomes, particularly in areas like law enforcement, credit scoring, and hiring.
- **Autonomous weapons:** The development of autonomous weapons systems that can operate without human intervention raises ethical and security concerns. These weapons could be used for malicious purposes or malfunction with devastating consequences.
- **Loss of control:** As AI systems become more complex and powerful, it is possible that we may lose control over them. This could lead to unintended consequences or even catastrophic outcomes.

Benefits and potential for good of AI:

- **Solving global challenges:** AI can be used to address some of the world's most pressing challenges, such as climate change, poverty, and disease. By automating tasks and analyzing large datasets, AI can help us to find more efficient and effective solutions.
- **Improving healthcare:** AI has the potential to revolutionize healthcare by providing more accurate diagnoses, personalized treatments, and improved patient care. AI can also be used to develop new drugs and therapies.
- **Enhancing human capabilities:** AI can be used to augment human intelligence and capabilities in various areas, such as education, research, and creative endeavors. This can lead to breakthroughs and innovations that would not be possible without AI.
- **Economic prosperity:** AI can drive economic growth and create new industries and jobs. By automating tasks and improving efficiency, AI can help businesses to be more productive and competitive.

Ultimately, whether AI is dangerous or beneficial depends on how it is developed and used. It is important to ensure that AI is developed responsibly and ethically, with safeguards in place to mitigate potential risks. We must also be mindful of the potential benefits of AI and work to ensure that it is used for the betterment of humanity.

It is important to consider the various perspectives on this issue and to engage in open and informed discussion about the future of AI. By working together, we can ensure that AI is used for good and not for harm.

EXAMPLE 2

Here is another example of a query submitted to Bard-3, followed by its detailed response:

User: What are some ways in which you can improve the accuracy of your responses to queries?

Bard: There are several ways to improve the accuracy of my responses to queries:

Data:

- **Larger and more diverse datasets:** Training on larger and more diverse datasets exposes me to a wider variety of language and information, improving my ability to generalize and generate accurate responses.
- **Higher quality data:** Focusing on data that is accurate, consistent, and relevant to specific tasks can significantly enhance my performance.
- **Domain-specific data:** Fine-tuning my training on datasets related to specific domains allows me to become an expert in those areas and provide more accurate and relevant responses.

Model Architecture:

- **More complex models:** Utilizing more sophisticated neural network architectures with greater depth and capacity can enable me to learn more complex relationships and generate more accurate outputs.
- **Ensemble models:** Combining predictions from multiple models can help to reduce bias and improve overall accuracy.
- **Model regularization techniques:** Techniques like dropout and weight decay can prevent overfitting and improve the generalizability of the model.

Training and Optimization:

- **Transfer learning:** Leveraging knowledge gained from pre-trained models on large datasets can significantly accelerate my learning process and improve performance on new tasks.
- **Multi-task learning:** Training me on multiple related tasks simultaneously can help me to learn more generalizable representations and improve performance across all tasks.
- **Active learning:** Focusing on learning from the most informative examples can significantly improve the efficiency and accuracy of the training process.

Evaluation and Feedback:

- **Human evaluation:** Regularly evaluating my responses through human feedback allows me to identify areas for improvement and prioritize the development of new capabilities.
- **Error analysis:** Analyzing common errors I make helps me to understand the causes of those errors and develop strategies to avoid them in the future.
- **Explainability and interpretability:** Developing techniques to explain my reasoning and the rationale behind my responses can help me to build trust and gain user confidence in my accuracy.

By continuously incorporating these strategies and advancements in AI and language modeling, I can strive to provide increasingly accurate and informative responses to your queries.

EXAMPLE 3

User: Can you give an example of an odd perfect number?
Bard: Unfortunately, it is not known whether odd perfect numbers exist. While there are infinitely many even perfect numbers, the existence of odd perfect numbers remains a mathematical problem with no confirmed solution.

Despite extensive research, no odd perfect number has been found yet. Mathematicians have proven several key properties related to odd perfect numbers, which provide some clues about their potential existence:

- **Odd perfect numbers must be greater than 10^1500.** This means that if an odd perfect number exists, it must be a very large number.
- **Odd perfect numbers are not divisible by 105.** This eliminates a large number of potential candidates from the search.
- **Odd perfect numbers must have the form $N \equiv 1$ (mod 12) or $N \equiv 117$ (mod 468) or $N \equiv 81$ (mod 324).** These congruences provide further restrictions on the possible forms of an odd perfect number.

While these properties offer valuable information, they haven't led to a definitive answer about the existence of odd perfect numbers. The search for them continues to be an active area of research in mathematics.

If you're interested in learning more about this fascinating mathematical problem, I encourage you to explore additional resources on odd perfect numbers. Here are some links that might be helpful:

- **Wikipedia article on odd perfect numbers:** *https://en.wikipedia.org/wiki/Perfect_number*
- **MathWorld article on odd perfect numbers:** *https://reference.wolfram.com/language/ref/PerfectNumber.html*
- **Numberphile video on odd perfect numbers:** *https://m.youtube.com/watch?v=0p1QsPRJcAU*

I hope this information is helpful!

EXAMPLE 4

User: Can you provide a proof of Goldbach's conjecture? Bard: Unfortunately, I cannot provide a complete proof of Goldbach's Conjecture at this time. While significant progress has been made towards proving it, a full and definitive proof remains elusive.

However, I can offer some information about the conjecture itself and the progress made towards proving it:

Goldbach's Conjecture: Every even integer greater than 2 can be expressed as the sum of two prime numbers.

Progress towards a proof:

- **Weak Goldbach's Conjecture:** Every odd integer greater than 5 can be expressed as the sum of three prime numbers. This was proven by Harald Helfgott in 2013.

- **Vinogradov's Theorem:** This theorem, proven in 1937, provided significant insights into the distribution of prime numbers and paved the way for further advancements in understanding Goldbach's Conjecture.
- **Chen Jingrun's Theorem:** This theorem, proven in 1966, showed that every sufficiently large even number can be expressed as the sum of a prime and the product of two primes.
- **Improvements on Chen's Theorem:** Numerous refinements and improvements have been made on Chen's Theorem, pushing the lower bound for sufficiently large even numbers even further.

Despite these advancements, complete proof for Goldbach's Conjecture still remains an open problem in mathematics. The complexity of the conjecture and the vastness of the number system make it an extremely challenging problem to tackle.

Here are some resources where you can find more information about Goldbach's Conjecture and the progress towards a proof:

- **Wikipedia article on Goldbach's Conjecture:** *https://simple.wikipedia.org/wiki/Goldbach%27s_conjecture*
- **MathWorld article on Goldbach's Conjecture:** *https://resources.wolframcloud.com/FunctionRepository/resources/Goldbach/*
- **Numberphile video on Goldbach's Conjecture:** *https://m.youtube.com/watch?v=MxiTG96QOxw*

While I cannot offer a complete proof at this time, I hope this information provides some insight into the fascinating world of Goldbach's Conjecture and the ongoing efforts to solve it.

EXAMPLE 5

User: Is there life after death, and how does it compare with life on Earth? Bard: The question of life after death is a profound one that has been pondered by humanity for millennia. There is no scientific consensus on the matter, as it is not something that can be directly observed or measured. However, various religions and philosophical perspectives offer different beliefs and theories about what, if anything, might exist beyond our physical lives.

Here are some of the major perspectives on life after death:

Religious Perspectives:

- **Abrahamic Religions:** Christianity, Islam, and Judaism all believe in some form of afterlife, where individuals are judged based on their actions in this life and rewarded or punished accordingly. The specific details of these afterlife realms vary across these religions.
- **Eastern Religions:** Hinduism, Buddhism, and Jainism believe in reincarnation, where the soul is reborn into another physical body after

death. The karma accumulated in previous lives determines the nature of the next life.

- **Indigenous Religions:** Many indigenous cultures around the world hold diverse beliefs about the afterlife, often involving the continuation of the spirit in a spiritual world or the interconnectedness of the living and the dead.

Philosophical Perspectives:

- **Materialism:** This view holds that consciousness is a product of the brain and ceases to exist after death. Therefore, there is no life after death in the traditional sense.
- **Dualism:** This view suggests that the mind and body are separate entities, with the mind potentially surviving the death of the body. This opens the possibility for some form of afterlife.
- **Near-Death Experiences (NDEs):** Some people who have had NDEs report experiencing a sense of peace, out-of-body experiences, and encounters with deceased loved ones. These experiences are often cited as evidence of an afterlife, but they can also be explained by physiological or psychological factors.

It is important to note that these are just a few of the many perspectives on life after death. Ultimately, the question of what, if anything, lies beyond our physical lives remains a mystery.

Comparing life after death with life on Earth is difficult, as we lack concrete information about what the afterlife might be like. However, based on various beliefs and theories, some potential differences include:

- **Immateriality:** In some afterlife scenarios, individuals may exist as noncorporeal beings, free from the limitations of a physical body.
- **Timelessness:** Time may not exist in the same way as it does on Earth, possibly allowing for experiences outside of our linear perception of time.
- **Knowledge and Understanding:** The afterlife may provide access to greater knowledge and understanding of the universe and ourselves.
- **Connections with Deceased Loved Ones:** Some beliefs suggest the possibility of reuniting with deceased loved ones in the afterlife.

Ultimately, the question of life after death is a personal one. Each individual must decide for themselves what they believe based on their own values, experiences, and understanding of the world.

It is important to respect diverse perspectives on this sensitive topic and avoid making claims of absolute certainty. While we may never have definitive answers about life after death, the continued exploration of this question can provide comfort, hope, and a sense of purpose for many.

Bard may display inaccurate info, including about people, so double-check its responses. Your privacy & Bard.

NOTE *As you can see from the preceding examples, Bard provides impressive and accurate responses to queries in a manner that surpasses many chatbots of recent years. However, it is still possible to confound this Bard (which is true of other chatbots as well).*

ALTERNATIVES TO BARD

There are several alternatives to Bard that offer a similar set of features, some of which are listed below:

- Bing Chat
- ChatGPT/GPT4
- Jasper
- PaLM (Google)
- Pi
- POE (LinkedIn)
- Replika
- WriteSonic
- YouChat

The following subsections discuss some (but not all) of the Bard alternatives in the preceding list.

YouChat

One alternative to Bard is YouChat, which is part of the search engine *you. com*. It is accessible at *https://you.com/*.

Richard Socher, who is well known in the ML community for his many contributions, is the creator of *you.com*. According to Socher, YouChat is a search engine that can provide the usual search-related functionality, as well as the ability to search the Web to obtain more information and provide responses to queries from users.

Another competitor is POE from LinkedIn, and you can create a free account at *https://poe.com/login*.

Pi from Inflection

Pi is a chatbot developed by Inflection, which is a company that was started by Mustafa Suleyman, who is also the founder of DeepMind. Pi is accessible at *https://pi.ai/talk*. More information about Pi can be found online:

https://medium.com/@ignacio.de.gregorio.noblejas/meet-pi-Bards-newest-rival-and-the-most-human-ai-in-the-world-367b461c0af1

The development team used Reinforcement Learning from Human Feedback (RLHF) in order to train this chatbot:

https://medium.com/@ignacio.de.gregorio.noblejas/meet-pi-chatgpts-newest-rival-and-the-most-human-ai-in-the-world-367b461c0af1

Shortly after the release of ChatGPT on November 30, 2022, there was a flurry of activity among various companies to release a competitor to ChatGPT, which arguably are also competitors to Bard, some of which are listed below:

- CoPilot (Microsoft)
- Codex (OpenAI)
- Apple GPT (Apple)
- Claude 2 (Anthropic)
- Llama-2 (Meta)

The following subsections contain additional details regarding the LLMs in the preceding list.

CoPilot (OpenAI/Microsoft)

Microsoft CoPilot is a Visual Studio Code extension that is also powered by GPT-4. GitHub CoPilot is already known for its ability to generate blocks of code within the context of a program. In addition, Microsoft is also developing Microsoft 365 CoPilot, whose availability date has not been announced as of mid-2023.

However, Microsoft has provided early demos that show some of the capabilities of Microsoft 365 CoPilot, which includes automating tasks such as

- writing emails
- summarizing meetings
- making PowerPoint presentations

Microsoft 365 CoPilot can analyze data in Excel spreadsheets, insert AI-generated images in PowerPoint, and generate drafts of cover letters. Microsoft has also integrated Microsoft 365 CoPilot into some of its existing products, such as Loop and OneNote.

According to the following article, Microsoft intends to charge $30 per month for Office 365 Copilot:

https://www.extremetech.com/extreme/microsoft-to-charge-30-per-month-for-ai-powered-office-apps

Copilot was reverse engineered in late 2022, which is described online:

https://thakkarparth007.github.io/copilot-explorer/posts/copilot-internals

The following article shows you how to create a GPT-3 application that uses NextJS, React, and CoPilot:

https://github.blog/2023-07-25-how-to-build-a-gpt-3-app-with-nextjs-react-and-github-copilot/

Codex (OpenAI)

OpenAI Codex is a fine-tuned GPT3-based LLM that generates code from text. Codex powers GitHub Copilot (discussed in the preceding section). Codex was trained on more than 150 GB of Python code that was obtained from more than 50 million GitHub repositories.

According to OpenAI, the primary purpose of Codex is to accelerate human programming, and it can complete almost 40% of requests. Codex tends to work quite well for generating code for solving simple tasks. Navigate to the Codex home page to obtain more information: *https://openai.com/blog/openai-codex*.

Apple GPT

In mid-2023, Apple announced Apple GPT, which is a competitor to Bard from OpenAI. The actual release date was projected to be 2024. "Apple GPT" is the current name for a product that is intended to compete with Google Bard, OpenAI Bard, and Microsoft Bing AI.

In brief, the LLM PaLM 2 powers Google Bard, and GPT-4 powers Bard as well as Bing Chat, whereas Ajax is what powers Apple GPT. Ajax is based on Jax from Google, and the name Ajax is a clever concatenation ("Apple Jax," perhaps?).

Claude 2

Anthropic created the LLM Claude 2. Claude 2 can not only answer queries about specific topics, but can also perform searches that involve multiple documents, summarize documents, create documents, and generate code.

Claude 2 is an improvement on Anthropic's predecessor Claude 1.3, and it can ingest entire books as well as generate code based on prompts from users. Claude 2 appears to be comparable with its rivals Bard and GPT-4 in terms of competing functionality.

Claude 2 supports a context window of 100,000 tokens. Moreover, Claude 2 was trained on data as recent as early 2023, whereas Bard was trained on data up until 2021. However, Claude 2 cannot search the Web (unlike its competitor GPT-4). Stay tuned to Anthropic, where you will probably see more good things in the LLM space.

SUMMARY

This chapter started with a discussion of generative AI, along with some of the major companies in this arena, such as Google, OpenAI, Cohere, and Hugging Face.

In addition, you learned about prompt engineering, which addresses the various ways that you can design the content of the prompts that you provide to an LLM.

Next, you learned about Google Gemini and some of its features, and read a brief comparison of Gemini Ultra with GPT-4 from OpenAI.

## CHAPTER 6

BARD AND PYTHON CODE

This chapter contains examples of using Bard to perform an eclectic mix of Python tasks, from generating Python code to scrape Web pages to generating code to calculate probabilities involved in throwing two or more dice. Bard generated all the code samples in this chapter. You can also submit your own prompts for Bard at this Web site:

https://bard.google.com/chat

https://blog.google/products/bard/google-bard-try-gemini-ai/

The first part of this chapter starts with details about uploading CSV files to Bard, along with Python code for handling text files and scraping Web sites.

The second part of this chapter contains Python code for creating a basic chatbot and performing data visualization. In addition, you will learn how to generate random numbers using Pandas.

The third part of this chapter introduces you to Fibonacci numbers, OOP (object-oriented programming), asynchronous programming, and how to work with the requests library in Python.

The fourth part of this chapter shows you how to use PIL for processing images and handling exceptions and includes an introduction to generators and decorators in Python. The final section of this chapter shows you how to calculate the probability of obtaining a certain number when rolling two, three, or four fair dice.

In general, the prompts that are used to generate the Python code samples have the following format:

```
Please generate Python code to render a [specific-graph-
name], along with an explanation of the Python code.
```

The prompts are very simple. They are a starting point, after which you can learn how to create more complex prompts for Bard.

CSV FILES FOR BARD

This section shows you how to make a CSV file available for Bard to generate Pandas and Python code samples. The following prompt asks Bard for information regarding how to upload a CSV file:

EXAMPLE 1

User: "How can I upload a CSV file?"

Bard: Unfortunately, I can't directly upload files or interact with external systems like websites or databases. However, I can help you with the general steps on how to upload a CSV file, depending on your specific situation.

To help me provide the most relevant information, please tell me:

Where are you trying to upload the CSV file? Is it a specific website, application, or software?

What platform are you using? Are you on a desktop computer, mobile device, or web browser?

Once I have this information, I can provide you with specific instructions on how to upload your CSV file.

EXAMPLE 2

User: "I would like to upload a CSV file from my laptop that you can use in order to generate Pandas code and Python code."

Bard: I'd be happy to help you with that! To generate Pandas and Python code from your CSV file, I need access to the data within the file. Here are a few ways you can share your CSV data with me:

1. Copy and paste the data:

   If your CSV file is small and the data fits comfortably in your clipboard, you can simply copy and paste the entire contents of the file into the chat box.

2. Upload the CSV file to a cloud storage service:

   You can upload your CSV file to a cloud storage service like Google Drive or Dropbox and share the public link with me.

3. Provide a link to the CSV file online:

   If your CSV file is publicly accessible online, you can simply share the URL with me.

   Once you have shared the data with me, I will be able to generate the requested Pandas and Python code. Please specify any additional information you want me to consider when generating the code, such as:

What kind of analysis are you trying to perform?
Are there any specific columns or rows you want to focus on?
What specific functionalities do you want the code to have?
The more information you provide, the better I can tailor the code to your specific needs.

The next section contains an example of Python code that Bard generated to scrape the contents of a Web page.

SIMPLE WEB SCRAPING

The Python code for the code sample in this section was generated via the following prompt for Bard:

```
Please generate Python code for scraping a Web page, along
with an explanation of the Python code.
```

Listing 6.1 displays the content of bard_web_scraping.py that Bard generated to perform Web scraping.

NOTE *Make sure you have installed the libraries* BeautifulSoup *and* requests, *which you can perform from the command line as follows:*

```
pip3 install bs4
pip3 install requests
```

LISTING 6.1: bard_web_scraping.py

```
import requests
from bs4 import BeautifulSoup

def scrape_titles(url):
    response = requests.get(url)
    soup = BeautifulSoup(response.content, 'html.parser')

    titles = []
    for title in soup.find_all('h2', class_='article-
title'):
        titles.append(title.text)

    return titles

# Usage
# titles = scrape_titles('https://dummywebsite.com/
articles')
# print(titles)
```

Listing 6.1 starts by importing requests and BeautifulSoup, followed by the function scrap_titles() that scrapes the contents of a given URL. This function initializes the variable response with the result of invoking the get() method with a given URL. Next, this function initializes the variable soup with the parsed contents of response.content.

The second part of this function contains a loop that iterates through all the <h2> HTML tags that also have a class attribute equal to article-title. For each such item, the text of the item is appended to the Python variable titles, which is initialized as an empty Python list. When the loop has completed, the code returns the variable titles, which consists of titles listed on the Web site.

The final portion of Listing 6.1 initializes the variable titles with the result of invoking scrape_titles() with a fictitious URL and then displays the result. Replace the fictitious URL with a valid URL, uncomment the final code snippets, and then check the generated output.

BASIC CHATBOT

The Python code for the code sample in this section was generated via the following prompt for Bard:

```
Please generate Python code for a basic chatbot, along with
an explanation of the Python code.
```

Listing 6.2 displays the content of bard_basic_chatbot.py that Bard generated to perform Web scraping.

LISTING 6.2: bard_basic_chatbot.py

```python
from bs4 import BeautifulSoup

def chatbot_response(text):
    responses = {
        'hello': 'Hi there!',
        'how are you': 'I am fine, thank you!',
        'bye': 'Goodbye!',
    }

    return responses.get(text.lower(), 'I am sorry, I do
not understand that.')

# Usage
response = chatbot_response('Hello')
print(response)   # Output: Hi there!
```

Listing 6.2 starts by importing BeautifulSoup, followed by the function chatbot_responses() that initializes the variable responses as a Python dictionary. The final portion of this function issues a return statement that converts the variable text to lowercase, and then the value associated with this lowercase string in the responses dictionary. If the string is not found, then a disclaimer type of message is returned.

The final portion of Listing 6.2 invokes the function `chatbot_response()` with the string `Hello`, which is a key in the `responses` dictionary. Launch the code in Listing 6.2, and you will see the output `Hi there!.`, which is the value associated with the key `Hello` in the `responses` dictionary.

BASIC DATA VISUALIZATION

The Python code for the code sample in this section was generated via the following prompt for Bard:

Please generate Python code for a simple data visualization, along with an explanation of the Python code.

Listing 6.3 displays the content of `bard_basic_visualization.py` that Bard generated to perform simple data visualization.

NOTE *For this task, you will need to have the* `matplotlib` *library installed as follows:*

```
pip3 install matplotlib
```

LISTING 6.3: bard_basic_visualization.py

```python
# Here's Python code for a simple data visualization using
the Matplotlib library:
import matplotlib.pyplot as plt

# Sample data
years = [2018, 2019, 2020, 2021, 2022]
temperatures = [14.5, 15.2, 16.1, 17.3, 18.2]

# Create the plot
plt.plot(years, temperatures)

# Add labels and title
plt.xlabel("Year")
plt.ylabel("Average Temperature (°C)")
plt.title("Average Temperature in a City from 2018 to
2022")

# Show the plot
plt.show()

"""
Explanation:
    Import library:
        We import the matplotlib.pyplot library as plt for
convenience.
```

```
     Sample data:
         We define two lists:
             years: A list of years from 2018 to 2022.
             temperatures: A list of average annual
temperatures for the corresponding years.

     Create the plot:
         plt.plot(years, temperatures) creates a line plot
with years on the x-axis and temperatures on the y-axis.

     Add labels and title:
         We use plt.xlabel, plt.ylabel, and plt.title to add
descriptive labels and a title to the plot.

     Show the plot:
         Finally, plt.show displays the generated plot on
the screen.

This code creates a basic line plot with minimal
formatting. Matplotlib offers various customization options
for further enhancing visualizations, such as:

     Changing plot styles and colors
     Adding grid lines and legend
     Adjusting axis limits and tick marks
     Creating different types of charts like bar charts,
scatter plots, and pie charts

You can explore the extensive Matplotlib documentation for
more information and tutorials on creating more complex and
visually appealing data visualizations.
"""
```

Launch the code in Listing 6.3, and you will see the line graph shown in Figure 6.1.

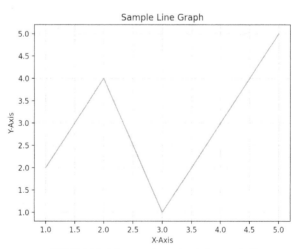

FIGURE 6.1 A line graph rendered via Matplotlib

BASIC PANDAS

Pandas is a powerful library for data manipulation. Be sure to install Pandas via the following command from the command line:

```
pip3 install pandas
```

The Python code for the code sample in this section was generated via the following prompt for Bard:

Please generate Python code to read a CSV file and then use Pandas in order to compute the mean of a column in the CSV file, along with an explanation of the Python code.

Listing 6.4 displays the content of bard_basic_pandas.py that Bard generated to read the contents of a CSV file and then compute the mean of a column in a subset of the rows of data.

LISTING 6.4: bard_basic_pandas.py

```python
# Python Code for Calculating Mean of a CSV Column with
Pandas
import pandas as pd

# Define the CSV file path
file_path = "your_file_path.csv"
file_path = "titanic.csv"

# Read the CSV file into a Pandas DataFrame
df = pd.read_csv(file_path)

# Choose the column to calculate the mean of
column_name = "your_column_name"
column_name = "age"

# Calculate the mean of the chosen column
mean = df[column_name].mean()

# Print the result
print(f"Mean of '{column_name}': {mean}")

"""
Explanation:

    Import library:
        We import the pandas library as pd for convenience.

    Define file path:
        Replace "your_file_path.csv" with the actual path to
your CSV file.

    Read CSV file:
```

```
        pd.read_csv(file_path) reads the CSV file into a
Pandas DataFrame named df.

    Choose column:
        Replace "your_column_name" with the name of the
column you want to calculate the mean of.

    Calculate mean:
        df[column_name].mean() calculates the mean of the
chosen column.

    Print result:
        The code prints a message showing the mean value
for the chosen column.


This code utilizes Pandas' functionalities to efficiently
read the CSV file, access specific columns, and perform
calculations on the data. It offers a clean and concise way
to analyze and extract insights from CSV files.
"""
```

Launch the code in Listing 6.4, and you will see the following single output line:

```
Mean of 'age': 29.8811345124283
```

GENERATING RANDOM DATA

In this section, we generate a list of random numbers and compute their mean and standard deviation. The Python code for the code sample in this section was generated via the following prompt for Bard:

```
Please generate Python code to generate a list of random
numbers and then compute their mean and standard deviation,
along with an explanation of the Python code.
```

Listing 6.5 displays the content of bard_random_numbers.py that Bard generated to create a set of random numbers and then display the contents of those numbers, as well as the mean and standard deviation of those numbers.

LISTING 6.5: bard_random_numbers.py

```
import random

# Define number of samples
num_samples = 100

# Generate random numbers
random_numbers = [random.random() for _ in range(num_samples)]
```

```
# Calculate mean
mean = sum(random_numbers) / num_samples

# Calculate standard deviation
variance = sum([(x - mean)**2 for x in random_numbers]) /
(num_samples - 1)
standard_deviation = variance**0.5

# Print results
print(f"Mean: {mean:.4f}")
print(f"Standard deviation: {standard_deviation:.4f}")

"""
```

Explanation:

Import library:
    We import the random library to access its random
number generator functions.

Define number of samples:
    num_samples specifies how many random numbers to
generate.

Generate random numbers:
    A list comprehension iterates num_samples times and
uses random.random() to generate random numbers between 0
and 1.

Calculate mean:
    We calculate the mean by summing all random numbers
and dividing by their total count.

Calculate variance and standard deviation:
    The code iterates over each number, calculates
its squared deviation from the mean, and then sums these
values.
    This sum is divided by num_samples - 1 to obtain
the unbiased sample variance.
    Finally, the square root of the variance is
calculated to get the standard deviation.

Print results:
    The code prints the mean and standard deviation
with four decimal places for better precision.

This code demonstrates how to generate random numbers and
compute their statistics using basic Python functions and
mathematical formulas. For more sophisticated statistical
analysis, you can explore other libraries like NumPy and
SciPy.
"""

Launch the code in Listing 6.5, and you will see the following type of output (your output will be slightly different):

```
Mean: 0.4532
Standard deviation: 0.2980
```

RECURSION: FIBONACCI NUMBERS

The Fibonacci sequence is a classic example of a problem that can be solved using recursion. Each Fibonacci number is the sum of the two preceding Fibonacci numbers.

The Python code for the code sample in this section was generated via the following prompt for Bard:

```
Please generate Python code to generate Fibonacci numbers,
along with an explanation of the Python code.
```

Listing 6.6 displays the contents of bard_fibonacci.py that shows you how to compute the n-th Fibonacci number using recursion.

LISTING 6.6: bard_fibonacci.py

```
# There are two common ways to generate Fibonacci numbers
in Python:
# 1. Recursive approach:

def fibonacci(n):
  """
  This function calculates the nth Fibonacci number
recursively.
  """
  if n <= 1:
    return n
  else:
    return fibonacci(n-1) + fibonacci(n-2)

# Generate the first 10 Fibonacci numbers
for i in range(10):
  print(fibonacci(i))


"""
Explanation:

    This code defines a function fibonacci(n) that takes an
integer n and returns the nth Fibonacci number.
    The base cases are n <= 1, where the nth Fibonacci
number is simply n.
    Otherwise, the function recursively calls itself with
n-1 and n-2 as arguments to calculate the previous two
Fibonacci numbers and sum them.
    The loop iterates from 0 to 9 and calls fibonacci(i) to
generate and print the first 10 Fibonacci numbers.
```

```
This approach is conceptually simple but can be inefficient
for large values of n due to repeated calculations.
"""

#2. Iterative approach:
def fibonacci(n):
    """
    This function calculates the nth Fibonacci number
iteratively.
    """
    a, b = 0, 1
    for i in range(n):
        a, b = b, a + b
    return a

# Generate the first 10 Fibonacci numbers
for i in range(10):
    print(fibonacci(i))

"""
Explanation:
    This code also defines a function fibonacci(n).
    It uses two variables, a and b, to store the previous
two Fibonacci numbers.
    The loop iterates n times, updating a and b by adding
them to get the next Fibonacci number.
    Finally, the function returns the value of a, which
represents the nth Fibonacci number.

This approach is more efficient for large values of n as it
avoids unnecessary repeated calculations.

Both approaches have their own advantages and
disadvantages. Choose the one that best suits your needs
and the size of the Fibonacci numbers you need to generate.
"""
```

Launch the code in Listing 6.6, and you will see the following list of Fibonacci numbers, where the first list of numbers was produced by the Python generator in Listing 6.6 and the second list of numbers was generated via an iterative solution:

```
0
1
2
3
5
8
13
21
34
0
1
1
2
```

```
3
5
8
13
21
34
```

GENERATING A PYTHON CLASS

The Python code for the code sample in this section was generated via the following prompt for Bard:

Please generate Python code to illustrate how to define a simple Python class, along with an explanation of the code.

Listing 6.7 displays the content of bard_python_oop.py that generates a rudimentary Python class that simulates two players who can score points.

LISTING 6.7: bard_python_oop.py

```python
class MyClass:
    """
    This is a simple Python class example.
    """

    # Class attributes
    name = "MyClass"
    version = 1.0

    # Constructor
    def __init__(self, attribute1, attribute2):
        self.attribute1 = attribute1
        self.attribute2 = attribute2

    # Method to print class information
    def print_info(self):
        print(f"Class name: {self.name}")
        print(f"Class version: {self.version}")
        print(f"Attribute 1: {self.attribute1}")
        print(f"Attribute 2: {self.attribute2}")

# Create an instance of the class
my_object = MyClass("Value 1", "Value 2")

# Access class attributes
print(f"Class name (attribute): {my_object.name}")

# Call class method
my_object.print_info()

"""
Explanation:
    Class definition:
```

The code starts by defining a class named MyClass
using the class keyword.
The class is documented with a docstring explaining
its purpose.
Class attributes:
Two class attributes are defined: name and
version. These attributes are shared by all instances of
the class.
Constructor:
The __init__ method is the constructor of the
class. It takes two arguments (attribute1 and attribute2)
and assigns them to instance attributes.
Class method:
A method named print_info is defined within the
class. This method can be used to print information about
the class and its attributes.
Creating an instance:
An instance of the MyClass class is created using
the MyClass constructor and assigning values to attribute1
and attribute2.
Accessing class attributes:
The name attribute of the my_object instance is
accessed and printed.
Calling class method:
The print_info method of the my_object instance
is called to print information about the class and its
attributes.

This example demonstrates the basic structure and
functionalities of a Python class. You can expand this example
by adding additional attributes, methods, and functionalities
to create more complex and sophisticated classes.
"""

Launch the code in Listing 6.7, and you will see the following output:

```
Class name (attribute): MyClass
Class name: MyClass
Class version: 1.0
Attribute 1: Value 1
Attribute 2: Value 2
```

ASYNCHRONOUS PROGRAMMING

This code sample demonstrates asynchronous programming by simulating two tasks running concurrently. The Python code for the code sample in this section was generated via the following prompt for Bard:

```
Please generate Python code to simulate two tasks running
simultaneously, along with an explanation of the Python
code.
```

Listing 6.8 displays the content of bard_async_example.py that Bard generated based on the preceding prompt.

LISTING 6.8: bard_async_example.py

```python
# Here are two ways to simulate two tasks running
simultaneously in Python:

import time
import threading

def task1():
  """
  Simulates a task that takes 2 seconds to complete.
  """
  print("Task 1 started")
  time.sleep(2)
  print("Task 1 finished")

def task2():
  """
  Simulates a task that takes 3 seconds to complete.
  """
  print("Task 2 started")
  time.sleep(3)
  print("Task 2 finished")

# Create and start threads
thread1 = threading.Thread(target=task1)
thread2 = threading.Thread(target=task2)

thread1.start()
thread2.start()

# Wait for both threads to finish
thread1.join()
thread2.join()

print("Both tasks finished!")

"""
Explanation:
    Imports:
        time is imported to introduce delays in the tasks.
        threading is imported to create and manage threads.
    Task functions:
        task1 and task2 are defined as functions that
simulate tasks taking 2 and 3 seconds, respectively.
    Creating threads:
        threading.Thread(target=task1) creates a thread
object that will run the task1 function when started.
        threading.Thread(target=task2) creates a thread
object that will run the task2 function when started.
    Starting threads:
        thread1.start() starts the thread object associated
with task1.
```

```
        thread2.start() starts the thread object associated
with task2.
    Joining threads:
        thread1.join() waits for the task1 thread to finish
before continuing.
        thread2.join() waits for the task2 thread to finish
before continuing.
    Finishing message:
        Once both threads have finished, a message is
printed.

This code demonstrates how to simulate two tasks running
simultaneously using Python threads. This allows you to
model concurrent processes and execute independent tasks
without blocking the main program flow.
"""
```

Launch the code in Listing 6.8, and you will see the following type of output:

```
Task 1 started
Task 2 started
Task 1 finished
Task 2 finished
Both tasks finished!
```

WORKING WITH REQUESTS IN PYTHON

The `requests` library provides an intuitive way to send HTTP requests. Here, we fetch data from a given API URL and extract a specific piece of information using the key.

The Python code for the code sample in this section was generated via the following prompt for Bard:

```
Please generate Python code to perform a Web request in
order to fetch the contents of a Web page, along with an
explanation of the Python code.
```

Listing 6.9 shows you the content of `bard_requests_example.py` that demonstrates Web API Interaction using the Python `requests` library to fetch data from an API and extract specific information.

LISTING 6.9: bard_requests_example.py

```python
import requests

def fetch_api_data(api_url, key):
    response = requests.get(api_url)
    response.raise_for_status()
    data = response.json()
    return data.get(key, None)
```

```
# Usage
# replace the fictitious URL with a real URL:
# result = fetch_api_data('https://api.sampleendpoint.com/
data', 'desired_key')
# print(result)
```

Listing 6.9 starts with an `import` statement, and then the `fetch_api()` function retrieves the contents of the specified URL. This function invokes the `get()` method and then initializes the variable data with the JSON-formatted `return` string.

The next portion of Listing 6.9 initializes the variable `result` with the `return` value from invoking the function `fetch_api_data()`. You must replace the fictitious URL with a valid URL and a legitimate value for `desired_key` before you can launch the code.

IMAGE PROCESSING WITH PIL

The Python Imaging Library (PIL) allows for a vast array of image processing tasks. The code sample in this section performs several transformations on the file `sample3.png`.

The Python code for the code sample in this section was generated via the following prompt for Bard:

Please generate Python code to perform image processing, along with an explanation of the Python code.

Listing 6.10 displays the content of `bard_image_processing.py` that shows you how to open an image, apply a grayscale filter, and save the result. (If you have not already done so, you need to install the `Pillow` library, a fork of PIL.)

LISTING 6.10: bard_image_processing.py

```
# Unfortunately, providing a general Python code for image
processing requires more information about the specific
task you want to achieve. Different image processing tasks
involve different libraries and techniques.

# However, I can provide an example of image processing
in Python using the PIL library to demonstrate the basic
workflow:
from PIL import Image

# Define the image path
image_path = "sample3.png"

# Open the image
image = Image.open(image_path)

# Convert the image to grayscale
grayscale_image = image.convert("L")
```

```
# Show the original and grayscale images
image.show()
grayscale_image.show()


"""
Explanation:
    Import library:
        We import the Image class from the PIL library for
image manipulation.

    Define image path:
        Replace "your_image_path.jpg" with the actual path
to your image file.

    Open image:
        Image.open(image_path) opens the image specified by
the path.

    Convert to grayscale:
        image.convert("L") converts the image to grayscale
mode.

    Show images:
        image.show() and grayscale_image.show() display the
original and grayscale images, respectively.
This is a simple example of image processing. You can use
PIL and other libraries like OpenCV to perform more complex
tasks such as:
    Applying filters and effects
    Detecting objects and features
    Segmenting images
    Generating new images
    Analyzing image statistics

To generate code for your specific image processing task,
please provide more details about the desired functionality
and the type of image manipulation you want to achieve.
"""
```

Launch the code in Listing 6.10, which generates the images shown in Figure 6.2 and Figure 6.3.

FIGURE 6.2 The original image.

Figure 6.3 displays the image that is generated by the second code block in Listing 6.13.

FIGURE 6.3 A gray scale image.

EXCEPTION HANDLING

Exception handling is crucial for robust programs. The Python code for the code sample in this section was generated via the following prompt for Bard:

Please generate Python code to perform exception handling, along with an explanation of the Python code.

In this example, we define a custom exception and showcase its usage and handling. Listing 6.11 shows you perform custom exception handling in Python.

LISTING 6.11: bard_exception_handling.py

```python
# Here is Python code demonstrating exception handling with
an explanation:
try:
    # Code that might raise an exception
    number = int(input("Enter a number: "))

    # Perform some operation with the number
    result = 10 / number
    print(f"Result: {result}")

except ValueError:
    # Handle invalid input
    print("Error: Please enter a valid number.")

except ZeroDivisionError:
    # Handle division by zero
    print("Error: Cannot divide by zero.")

finally:
    # Always execute this block, regardless of exceptions
    print("This block is always executed.")
"""
```

```
Explanation:
    try block:
        This block contains the code that might raise an
exception.
        In this case, we read a user input and attempt to
convert it to an integer.

    except blocks:
        These blocks handle specific exceptions that may
occur within the try block.
        The except ValueError block handles cases where the
user input cannot be converted to an integer.
        The except ZeroDivisionError block handles cases where
the user enters 0 as input, resulting in division by zero.
        Each except block can define its own code to handle
the specific exception.

    finally block:
        This block always executes, regardless of whether
an exception occurs or not.
        It is often used to perform cleanup tasks or close
resources opened in the try block.

This code demonstrates basic exception handling in Python.
You can use different exception types and provide more
specific handling logic for each case depending on your
needs. Remember to use appropriate try/except blocks to
handle potential errors and ensure your code runs robustly
under different conditions.
" " "
```

Launch the code in Listing 6.11, and you will see the following output.

```
Caught an exception: This is a custom exception!
```

GENERATORS IN PYTHON

Generators allow for lazy evaluation, producing values on-the-fly without storing the entire sequence in memory. The Python code for the code sample in this section was generated via the following prompt for Bard:

```
Please generate Python code that uses a Python generator
in order to generate Fibonacci numbers, along with an
explanation of the Python code.
```

Listing 6.12 shows you the content of bard_generator_fibonacci.py that shows you how to define a generator that produces Fibonacci numbers in Python.

LISTING 6.12: bard_generator_fibonacci.py

```
def fibonacci_generator(): # see comment below
    " " "
```

```
   Generates Fibonacci numbers using a generator function.

   This function implements the Fibonacci sequence using a
generator function. It avoids
   storing all the calculated Fibonacci numbers in memory,
making it more efficient
   for large values.

   Yields:
     Each consecutive Fibonacci number.
   """
   a, b = 0, 1
   while True:
     yield a
     a, b = b, a + b

# Example usage
fib_numbers = fibonacci_generator()

for _ in range(10):
  print(next(fib_numbers))
```

Launch the code in Listing 6.12, and you will see the following output:

```
0
1
1
2
3
5
8
13
21
34
```

One interesting observation is that the first time that Bard was prompted to generate the code in Listing 6.12, the first line of code passed a parameter to the function, as shown here:

```
def fibonacci_generator(n):
```

The code with the preceding code snippet returned only the value 0 for each Fibonacci number. However, when the same prompt was submitted a second time, the correct code was generated. Although Bard generates correct code most of the time (in fact, all the other code samples for this book are correct), you might encounter a similar situation.

ROLL 7 OR 11 WITH TWO DICE

This section contains a dialogue with Bard to determine the probability of rolling a 7 or an 11 with two balanced dice. The explanation was generated via the following prompt for Bard:

User: Suppose that I toss two fair dice and I win if the sum of the values is either 7 or 11. What is the probability that I will win and please provide an explanation.

Bard: To solve this problem, we need to calculate the probability of rolling a 7 or 11 with two fair dice.

There are a total of 36 possible outcomes when rolling two dice, as each die has 6 sides and any combination of their values can occur.

Calculating the probability of rolling 7:

There are 6 ways to roll a sum of 7:

1 + 6
2 + 5
3 + 4
4 + 3
5 + 2
6 + 1

Therefore, the probability of rolling a 7 is:

$P(7)$ = Number of ways to roll 7 / Total number of outcomes = 6 / 36

Calculating the probability of rolling 11:

There are 2 ways to roll a sum of 11:

5 + 6
6 + 5

Therefore, the probability of rolling a 11 is:

$P(11)$ = Number of ways to roll 11 / Total number of outcomes = 2 / 36

Calculating the probability of winning:

As we win if we roll either a 7 or 11, we need to add the probabilities of those two events.

$P(winning) = P(7) + P(11)$
$P(winning) = 6/36 + 2/36$
$P(winning) = 8/36$

Therefore, the probability of winning is 8/36, which can be simplified to 2/9.

ROLL 7 OR 11 WITH THREE DICE

This section contains a dialogue with Bard to determine the probability of rolling a 7 or an 11 with three balanced dice. The explanation was generated via the following prompt for Bard:

User: Suppose that I toss three fair dice and I win if the sum of the values is either 7 or 11. What is the probability that I will win and please provide an explanation.

Bard: To calculate the probability of winning in this scenario, we need to consider the number of winning outcomes and compare it to the total number of possible outcomes when rolling three dice.

Calculating the total number of outcomes: Each die has 6 sides, and when rolling three dice, each side of one die can be combined with any side of the other two dice. Therefore, the total number of possible outcomes is:

Total outcomes = 6^3 = 216

Calculating the number of winning outcomes: There are two winning scenarios: rolling a sum of 7 or rolling a sum of 11.

Rolling a sum of 7: There are 15 ways to roll a sum of 7:

$$1 + 1 + 5$$
$$1 + 2 + 4$$
$$1 + 3 + 3$$
$$1 + 4 + 2$$
$$1 + 5 + 1$$
$$2 + 1 + 4$$
$$2 + 2 + 3$$
$$2 + 3 + 2$$
$$2 + 4 + 1$$
$$3 + 1 + 3$$
$$3 + 2 + 2$$
$$3 + 3 + 1$$
$$4 + 1 + 2$$
$$4 + 2 + 1$$
$$5 + 1 + 1$$

Rolling a sum of 11: There are 27 ways to roll a sum of 11:

$$1 + 5 + 5$$
$$1 + 6 + 4$$
$$2 + 4 + 5$$
$$2 + 5 + 4$$
$$2 + 6 + 3$$
$$3 + 3 + 5$$
$$3 + 4 + 4$$
$$3 + 5 + 3$$
$$3 + 6 + 2$$
$$4 + 2 + 5$$
$$4 + 3 + 4$$
$$4 + 4 + 3$$
$$4 + 5 + 2$$
$$4 + 6 + 1$$
$$5 + 1 + 5$$
$$5 + 2 + 4$$
$$5 + 3 + 3$$
$$5 + 4 + 2$$

$$5 + 5 + 1$$
$$6 + 1 + 4$$
$$6 + 2 + 3$$
$$6 + 3 + 2$$
$$6 + 4 + 1$$
$$6 + 5 + 5$$
$$6 + 6 + 6$$

Calculating the probability of winning: We need to determine the total number of winning outcomes and divide it by the total number of possible outcomes.

Total winning outcomes = Number of ways to roll 7 + Number of ways to roll 11 = 15 + 27 = 42
Probability of winning = Total winning outcomes / Total number of outcomes = 42/216
P(winning) = 7/36

Therefore, the probability of winning in this scenario is 7/36.

ROLL 7 OR 11 WITH FOUR DICE

This section contains a dialogue with Bard to determine the probability of rolling a 7 or an 11 with four balanced dice. The explanation was generated via the following prompt for Bard:

User: Suppose that I toss four fair dice and I win if the sum of the values is either 7 or 11. What is the probability that I will win and please provide an explanation.

Bard: Solving this problem requires calculating the probability of getting a sum of 7 or 11 when rolling four dice.

Total Possible Outcomes: Each die has 6 sides and rolling four dice results in 6 * 6 * 6 * 6 = 1296 possible outcomes.

Winning Outcomes:

1. Sum of 7:

There are 21 ways to get a sum of 7:

$$1 + 1 + 1 + 4$$
$$1 + 1 + 2 + 3$$
$$1 + 1 + 3 + 2$$
$$1 + 2 + 1 + 3$$
$$1 + 2 + 2 + 2$$
$$1 + 3 + 1 + 2$$
$$1 + 3 + 2 + 1$$
$$2 + 1 + 1 + 3$$
$$2 + 1 + 2 + 2$$

$$2 + 2 + 1 + 2$$
$$3 + 1 + 1 + 2$$
$$3 + 1 + 2 + 1$$
$$4 + 1 + 1 + 1$$

2. Sum of 11:

There are 39 ways to get a sum of 11:

$$1 + 5 + 5 + 5$$
$$1 + 6 + 4 + 4$$
$$1 + 6 + 5 + 3$$
$$2 + 4 + 5 + 5$$
$$2 + 5 + 4 + 5$$
$$2 + 5 + 5 + 4$$
$$2 + 6 + 3 + 4$$
$$2 + 6 + 4 + 3$$
$$3 + 3 + 5 + 5$$
$$3 + 4 + 4 + 5$$
$$3 + 4 + 5 + 4$$
$$3 + 5 + 3 + 5$$
$$3 + 5 + 4 + 4$$
$$3 + 5 + 5 + 3$$
$$3 + 6 + 2 + 4$$
$$3 + 6 + 3 + 3$$
$$3 + 6 + 4 + 2$$
$$4 + 2 + 5 + 5$$
$$4 + 3 + 4 + 5$$
$$4 + 3 + 5 + 4$$
$$4 + 4 + 3 + 5$$
$$4 + 4 + 4 + 4$$
$$4 + 4 + 5 + 3$$
$$4 + 5 + 2 + 5$$
$$4 + 5 + 3 + 4$$
$$4 + 5 + 4 + 3$$
$$5 + 1 + 5 + 5$$
$$5 + 2 + 4 + 5$$
$$5 + 2 + 5 + 4$$
$$5 + 3 + 3 + 5$$
$$5 + 3 + 4 + 4$$
$$5 + 3 + 5 + 3$$
$$5 + 4 + 2 + 5$$
$$5 + 4 + 3 + 4$$
$$5 + 4 + 4 + 3$$
$$5 + 5 + 1 + 5$$
$$5 + 5 + 2 + 4$$
$$5 + 5 + 3 + 3$$

Total Winning Outcomes:

Adding the winning outcomes for both sums: 21 + 39 = 60

Probability of Winning:

Divide the total winning outcomes by the total possible outcomes:

P(winning) = 60 / 1296 = 5 / 108

Therefore, the probability of winning in this scenario is 5/108.

Solving this problem requires calculating the probability of getting a sum of 7 or 11 when rolling four dice.

Total Possible Outcomes:

Each die has 6 sides and rolling four dice results in 6 * 6 * 6 * 6 = 1296 possible outcomes.

Winning Outcomes:

1. Sum of 7:

    There are 21 ways to get a sum of 7:

    > 1 + 1 + 1 + 4
    > 1 + 1 + 2 + 3
    > 1 + 1 + 3 + 2
    > 1 + 2 + 1 + 3
    > 1 + 2 + 2 + 2
    > 1 + 3 + 1 + 2
    > 1 + 3 + 2 + 1
    > 2 + 1 + 1 + 3
    > 2 + 1 + 2 + 2
    > 2 + 2 + 1 + 2
    > 3 + 1 + 1 + 2
    > 3 + 1 + 2 + 1
    > 4 + 1 + 1 + 1

2. Sum of 11:

    There are 39 ways to get a sum of 11:

    > 1 + 5 + 5 + 5
    > 1 + 6 + 4 + 4
    > 1 + 6 + 5 + 3
    > 2 + 4 + 5 + 5
    > 2 + 5 + 4 + 5
    > 2 + 5 + 5 + 4
    > 2 + 6 + 3 + 4
    > 2 + 6 + 4 + 3
    > 3 + 3 + 5 + 5
    > 3 + 4 + 4 + 5

$$3 + 4 + 5 + 4$$
$$3 + 5 + 3 + 5$$
$$3 + 5 + 4 + 4$$
$$3 + 5 + 5 + 3$$
$$3 + 6 + 2 + 4$$
$$3 + 6 + 3 + 3$$
$$3 + 6 + 4 + 2$$
$$4 + 2 + 5 + 5$$
$$4 + 3 + 4 + 5$$
$$4 + 3 + 5 + 4$$
$$4 + 4 + 3 + 5$$
$$4 + 4 + 4 + 4$$
$$4 + 4 + 5 + 3$$
$$4 + 5 + 2 + 5$$
$$4 + 5 + 3 + 4$$
$$4 + 5 + 4 + 3$$
$$5 + 1 + 5 + 5$$
$$5 + 2 + 4 + 5$$
$$5 + 2 + 5 + 4$$
$$5 + 3 + 3 + 5$$
$$5 + 3 + 4 + 4$$
$$5 + 3 + 5 + 3$$
$$5 + 4 + 2 + 5$$
$$5 + 4 + 3 + 4$$
$$5 + 4 + 4 + 3$$
$$5 + 5 + 1 + 5$$
$$5 + 5 + 2 + 4$$
$$5 + 5 + 3 + 3$$

Total Winning Outcomes:
Adding the winning outcomes for both sums: $21 + 39 = 60$
Probability of Winning:
Divide the total winning outcomes by the total possible outcomes:

$P(\text{winning}) = 60 / 1296 = 5 / 108$

Therefore, the probability of winning in this scenario is 5/108.

MEAN AND STANDARD DEVIATION

Please calculate the mean and standard deviation of the numbers in the set $S = \{9, 2, -8, 17, 4, 37\}$ and please provide details.

Listing 6.16 shows you the content of `bard_mean_std.py` that Bard generated to calculate the mean and standard deviation of a set of numbers.

LISTING 6.16: bard_mean_std.py

```
import numpy as np

#Please generate Python code that calculates the mean and
standard deviation of the numbers in the set S = {9,2,
-8,17,4,37} and please provide details.

# Define the set S
S = {9, 2, -8, 17, 4, 37}

# Import statistics library
import statistics

# Calculate the mean
mean = statistics.mean(S)
print(f"Mean: {mean}")

# Calculate the standard deviation
std_dev = statistics.stdev(S)
print(f"Standard deviation: {std_dev}")

"""
Explanation:
    Import library:
        We import the statistics library which provides
functions for calculating various statistics.
    Define set:
        We define the set S containing the given numbers.
    Calculate mean:
        We use the statistics.mean(S) function to calculate
the average of all elements in the set.
    Calculate standard deviation:
        We use the statistics.stdev(S) function to
calculate the standard deviation of the elements in the
set.
    Print results:
        We print the calculated mean and standard deviation
with descriptive messages.

This code provides a concise and efficient way to calculate
the mean and standard deviation of a set in Python.
"""
```

Launch the code in Listing 6.16, and you will see the following output:

```
Mean: 10.166666666666666
Standard deviation: 15.510211689937268
```

SUMMARY

This chapter contains Python-based solutions generated by Bard to a variety of tasks. The first set of tasks involved tasks such as Web scraping and file-based operations.

Then you learned about data visualization using a popular open-source Python-based library called Matplotlib. In addition, you learned how to use recursion to calculate Fibonacci numbers, followed by an example that uses a generator to calculate Fibonacci numbers.

You also saw an example of how to interact with Bard to debug a code sample that was generated by Bard in Listing 6.10 and Listing 6.11.

In addition, you learned how to perform image processing in Python that involved multiple transformations on a PNG file. You saw how to define custom exception handlers in Python, as well as how to work with generators in Python.

You saw how to calculate the mean and the standard deviation of a set of numbers. Finally, you learned how to calculate probabilities of obtaining a given number by tossing 2, 3, or 4 well-balanced dice.